The Work Goes On

Another week in the life of a substance abuse counselor

A Novel by

Mary Crocker Cook, D.Min., LMFT, LPCC, LAADC, CADCII

The Work Goes On

© 2015 Mary Crocker Cook

ISBN: 978-1-61170-197-5

All rights reserved. No part of this publication may be reproduced, stored in a retrieval system or transmitted in any form or by any means, electronic, mechanical, photocopies, recording or otherwise, without the prior written consent of the author.

Published in the USA.

Robertson Publishing™
www.RobertsonPublishing.com

Printed in the USA, UK, and Australia on acid-free paper.

To purchase additional copies go to:
 amazon.com
 barnesandnoble.com

The Work Goes On is the second in a two part series written because I fell in love with the staff in the first novel, and needed to see what they were up to! It is a product of my imagination and in no way depicts specific counselors and staff from my treatment center experience. The characters are a composite, and I suspect will be familiar to those who share my love of treatment and alcohol and drug counselors.

I have provided a weekly schedule for readers who may be unfamiliar with the day-to-day structure of treatment. As you are reading you might be struck by the pace of the day, and I assure you this pace is very real! I have also illustrated specific groups that take place during the week to provide a window into the treatment world.

With many thanks to my editor, Howard Scott Warshaw, LMFT

—Mary Crocker Cook

The Work Goes On

Prologue

Janet's voice is muffled by the pillow, "I don't understand what you're asking me."

Her therapist thinks a moment. "What's the payoff for hanging on?"

Janet peeks an eye up through the pillow fringe, "You want to know what's in it for me to stay stuck – to stay dead inside."

The room is quiet.

Janet covers her chest with the pillow as she sits up. "I'm afraid – what if this happens again? I don't think I could do this again… there are so many bimbos in the world. I can't compete." Janet says with tears in her eyes.

"What if you didn't have to? What if you choose someone who would never compare you? Would feel blessed to have you?"

"I can't picture that."

"I wonder if you're willing to HANDLE that?" her therapist challenges.

Janet just stared at her, and the start of a grin flitted across her face.

"So maybe I'm using David's abandonment as an excuse – I chose someone emotionally unavailable so I never had to fully ante up?"

"It's something to think about," her therapist mulls aloud.

The Work Goes On

Daily Schedule

	M	T	W	TH	F	Sat	Sun
7:00-8:30	Wake/brkfst	Wake/brkfst	Wake/brkfst	Wake/brkfst	Wake/brkfst	Wake/brkfst	Wake/brkfst
8:30-9:00	Mindfulness	Mind.	Mind.	Mind.	Mind.	Mind.	Mind.
9:00-10:00	Women/Men's Group	Yoga	Nutrition	DBT	Assignment Group	Family only	Free
10:15-11:00	Comm Group	Comm. Group	Comm. Group	Comm. Group	Comm. Group	10:30-11:45 Multi-family	Double Scrub
11:30-12:30	Psychoed	Psych'd	Psych'd	Psych'd	Psych	12:00 Lunch	
12:30-1:45	Lunch/Staff mtg	Lunch	Lunch	Lunch	Lunch	Visit	Lunch
2:00-3:30	Process Group	Process	Process	Art Therapy	Process	Visit	
3:30-5:00	Free					3:00 Visiting over	4:00 Outside meeting
5:00-6:00	Dinner						
6:00-6:30	After Dinner clean-up						Dinner
6:30-8:00	Psychoed	Psych'd	Psych'd	Psych'd	Psych'd	H&I Meeting	
8:00-9:00	Chores	Chores	Chores	Chores	Chores	Chores	Chore
9:00-11:00	Free						

The Work Goes On

MONDAY

Janet, the lead counselor, continues to struggle with the loss of her long-time partner who dumped her for a bimbo. Even several years later Janet continues to be weighed down by a deadness inside. *"She may be right,"* Janet ponders as she heads to work. *"Thank God I can go do something useful with my cowardly ass,"* she thinks as she pulls into the treatment center.

As she enters the office she sees Keisha shepherding the clients into breakfast, and dragging the dawdlers out of bed so they'll be on time for morning Mindfulness. Janet watches her from the doorway, and is struck by Keisha's bearing. *"She's so graceful,"* she thinks. *"She carries herself with such dignity, such a quiet presence. No wonder the clients respond so well to her, even when she pushes them to follow the structure they fight."* Janet waves to her and receives a glowing smile.

Her clients have spotted her arrival, and begin to cluster around her desk. She pokes her head through the group to greet Ricardo who is managing his own client line up. "Morning Bubba!" she grins. "Mamacita!" he nods.

Jason is first up, anxious about the letter he will need for court next week. Janet reassures him that there is plenty of time and that he will have what he needs. One of the challenges of working in residential treatment is the chronic presence of poor impulse control. So many of the clients display the arrested development of early alcohol and drug use and so function in the moment. The executive functions of long term planning, impulse control and organization are often impaired in early recovery and there's an urgency to their thoughts and needs that one would normally see in an adolescent.

One of the reasons so many recovering people work in treatment is that their life experience gives them patience with this urgency, recognizing it as an artifact of a long term disease versus a personality or character trait. This same trait is particularly vexing for family members who see a 30 year old man and get caught up in the chaos of 16 year old decision making.

Cathy is standing in front of Janet, shifting from foot to foot.

"Good morning, Cathy. How can I help you?"

"I need to use the phone, and I'm still on phone restriction," she says.   Residents are often on phone restriction when they first enter residential treatment to allow them to focus and integrate into their new surroundings. Outside drama and worry can be compelling and sabotage someone's treatment episode.

"I can help you with that if the call is business. What do you need?" Janet asks.

"My mom forgot to bring me the jeans I wanted her to bring on Family Day. I really want to wear them."

"Do you have enough clothes to wear?" Janet asks

"I want to wear THOSE when we go to outside meetings," Cathy explains peevishly.

"Well, you are in luck! We go to outside meetings on Sunday, after Family day. So you can call her Friday and remind her to bring them. How about that?" Janet proposes.

Cathy frowns, and turns to leave. "Whatever," which is universal adolescent speak for F**k you! Janet smiles to herself and says to Ricardo, "It's only 8:45 and I have already been told to F**k off. Happy Monday!" Janet laughs.

"Wanna do Community group with me this morning?" Ricardo offers.

"You know, I would. I need to see the mood of the house. I'll join you after women's group."

Ricardo gives her a fist bump on the way to lead men's group.

Women's Group

Janet looks around the room, watching the body language of the women, and notes that Cathy has pulled her hoodie up. Janet catches her eye and gestures for her to put it down, which Cathy does begrudgingly. Hoodies and hats are often not allowed in counseling sessions due to the fact they obscure the client's face and make it hard to connect with them.

Lonnie checks in first. "I really had a hard time with my husband this Saturday. Actually, he had to leave early and I was relieved. Then I felt guilty. . ." she opens.

"What was the hardest part for you?" Janet wonders.

"He's so angry at me, so judgmental. He brings up how much the treatment is costing us every time we talk, and lets me know every night how much he's struggling with our daughters. I swear he thinks I'm in here getting some kind of spa treatment!" she says heatedly.

"I know for sure that's what my Mom thinks," Alicia agrees. "She even says things like, 'While you're roosted up in there with your new friends,' or "It's nice to see you have so much time to yourself' after she points out what a pain in the ass the traffic is when she picks up my son."

"How do you manage the guilt tripping?" Jane asks.

"I try not to listen to it but honestly it makes me angry, and ashamed," Alicia admits.

Lonnie nods. "I can relate. I act like I'm blowing him off but it hurts."

"Have you thought about being honest with them about how their words hit you?" Janet says.

"Honestly, I feel like he has a point. I DID get arrested for forging the prescription, and I DID leave him alone with the girls" Lonnie says. "I probably deserve it."

"He definitely has been impacted by your using, and I am sure the legal costs and costs of treatment feel really large right now." Janet acknowledges. "At the same time, addiction is a disease, not a hobby, and part of healing is learning to be emotionally honest and not build resentments we eventually use over.

Maybe we can talk more in our one-on-ones about ways you could approach your husband the next time he guilts you."

Lonnie nods. "I need help with this."

"Actually it sounds like you need permission," Donna throws in.

"Great point!" Janet grins. "Donna, how do you know?"

"Because I've been talking to my old sponsor, and she told me that when I was afraid to tell my girlfriend that I needed to leave the relationship. I didn't want to be the bad guy," she explains.

"So you just drank and used to drive her away?" Janet asks.

"Like I heard from someone, 'drink the poison hoping they will die,' " Donna grins.

Janet grins back, "I so get that!"

Janet pops back into the office to check her messages before community group with Ricardo. She hears a quick rap on the door and sees Alan standing there holding a towel.

"Hi, Alan. What's with the towel?"

"I didn't have a chance to shower before mindfulness and I want to take a shower instead of going to community group" he asks.

"So, what happened with your shower? Did you get up late?" Janet asks.

Alan is quiet a moment. "It's that guy, Tony. He uses all the hot water and stays in there 30 minutes at least. When I knock on the door he tells me to 'F**k off,' sorry for my language."

Janet nods. "Have you talked to him about it at any other time, or asked for staff help?" she asks.

"I didn't want to be a snitch. I don't want to get him in trouble, I just want a shower."

Conflict is so hard for recovering folks. They either start out aggressively to prevent any conflict, or stuff their feelings and drink. Being assertive and direct can feel like a foreign language. In some cases, speaking up may have led to childhood violence, and staying quiet may have been a smart survival tactic.

"Alan, I'm going to challenge you to bring this issue up in Community group. You don't have to confront Tony directly, but can bring up the shower time issue. I think it would be good practice for you. Besides, you'll have me as back up," she smiles.

Alan looks very reluctant. "I shouldn't have said anything," he says regretfully.

"Alan, look, this is the kind of situation we use over. It's the small shit that pushes us over the cliff. Ever notice that?" she asks. 'I'm going to ask you to trust me that this is the kind of skill that'll keep you sober in the long run."

Alan nods. "Okay," he says with reluctance. "I'll give it a try."

"I've got your back," she laughs as she follows him to group.

Community Group

Ricardo, Janet, Keisha the Chemical Dependency (CD) Tech, and Jesse the CD Intern lead off community group, an hour long "house meeting" that allows the residents to give each other feedback, express appreciation and concerns, and lets the counselors know what might be needed for the household. Everyone goes around the circle with a one feeling word check-in then the group is opened up for concerns. Janet looks pointedly at Alan.

"I have a concern," Alan opens. "The hot water is running out in the morning, and I didn't get to take a hot shower this morning. Is there a time limit on showers?" he asks.

"Is this about me?" Tony asks aggressively.

"It's about hot water, dude. It's not personal," Alan responds.

"There actually IS a fifteen minute shower rule," Keisha

The Work Goes On

acknowledges. "I have had a hard time tracking this because you guys aren't getting up on time, so I get caught up trying to get you to breakfast, "she says with some resentment.

"That sounds exhausting, Keisha. How did it become your job to wake the clients up?"

"Well, if I don't they'll be late to class," she observes.

"Then what?" Ricardo asks.

"Well, I guess they would get a consequence of some kind," she starts to smile.

"Exactly!" Janet says. She turns to the group. "Keisha's working harder on your program than you guys are. I am going to encourage her to let YOU be in charge of wake up – you all have alarm clocks. If it would help, we could put egg-timers in the bathroom because I know that following structure is still new for a lot of you."

"Yeah," says Angie. "I'm used to tweaker hours!" she laughs and everyone laughs with her.

As the group is breaking up Janet catches Alan's eyes and gives him a thumbs up. He blushes and wanders off to the kitchen.

Janet is reviewing the log balancing a cruller in one hand and coffee in the other when Keisha enters the room. As the door opens, Janet hears the clients talking in Ricardo's psycho-education group and she smiles. "Dude's getting better," she thinks, "They get to talk too!"

"Janet, can we talk for a minute?" Keisha asks.

Janet looks up from the log and gestures to the chair by her desk with her coffee hand. "Please, join me. What's up?"

"I was really embarrassed when you fronted me off in front of the clients like that. It hurt my feelings."

Janet is surprised, but thinks a minute. "You mean about the wake up thing?" she clarifies.

"Yeah. I felt stupid."

"Wow, Keisha, I'm so sorry I disrespected you like that. I certainly didn't mean to. Now that I think about it, I was on a roll and trying to make a point to the clients. I didn't even THINK about how what I was saying might make you feel."

"I get it, it wasn't personal."

"No ma'am it wasn't, but it was stupid. What I was actually thinking, in my inside voice, is that I was going to bring up the idea of covering for people or taking on other people's responsibility as a relapse trigger during Process group this afternoon. So, I was planting a seed, so to speak, though I can see where I could have been way more tactful."

"How did you learn to think in so many layers?" Keisha wonders.

"I am long in the tooth, honey, and have learned to think in terms of group issues. To me, the house is the client, not just the individual, and so I am always looking for house themes. Does that make sense?"

"Yeah, it does. I was thinking that maybe I might take some classes. What do you think?"

"Keisha, I think you would be a natural. In fact, I was admiring your rapport with the clients this morning when I came in. I think you should do it."

"Well, Jesse is almost done and I can see how much he's learned. I'm seeing that there's way more to this job than just sharing my own experience, strength, and hope. It's a job!"

Janet grins. "It is a calling, actually, if you know what I mean."

Keisha

Keisha does know what Janet means. She has 4 years clean from crack cocaine use, and comes from a large family of addicts and alcoholics. She was the third person in her family to get clean, so has the support of her sober Dad and clean brother. However, she spends a great deal of her energy worrying about the family members who are still loaded and in and out of custody. Keisha decided to stop using during an 8-month stay in the local jail where she attended a women's in-custody treatment program. She paid attention to the women in her group who had been to jail over and over again, and recognized their weathered and hopeless faces as the Aunts and Uncles in her own family. It was the ghost of Christmas future, and it scared her. She made the decision to "get a life" and re-enter the world as a recovering person when she was discharged. She still has a year left on her probation, so is not eligible to be a CD counselor. She has to discharge before she can be hired in a counselor role, so now is a good time to go to school.

Janet hears the squeaking of chairs that indicates that the Psycho-education group breaking up, and Ricardo enters the room. He looks pleased with himself, which tickles Janet.

"Hey, Ricardo, we got a fax that we are getting a new state guy tomorrow. I'm taking Brian, the new guy, so he's yours."

"Oh, are you sure? I know how much you love the prison guys… the conning… the scheming… the plotting," he grins.

"Yeah. Tempting as it is, he's yours."

"That's cool. I like working with those guys. They keep me on my toes!" he laughs.

Clinical Staffing

The Clinical Director enters the room in preparation for Clinical Staffing, and grabs the log book to get up to speed. He nods at Janet and Ricardo, who turn to greet Jesse, the weekend CD Tech/Intern who is easily identified by the intrusive Harley sounds as he rides up. He hustles in with Taco Bell today, and grabs a chair. Sarah, the former Intern, now Chemical Dependency (CD) Tech comes in with Eddie, the evening counselor who fist bumps everyone in the room. Carl, the night CD Tech wanders in drowsily, with Kym the Family counselor and Jorge the CD Tech trailing behind.

Jesse is playing two roles right now, because he's working Internship hours Monday and Thursday during the week for his last semester of practicum, and is still the weekend CD Tech. Wearing both hats has been a role strain for him, and he opens the group with a concern left over from the weekend.

"Guys, can I start? I need to get some feedback," Jesse opens. "I had this weird experience over the weekend with Jeff. He's on my caseload for my Internship and I have been doing his one-on-ones with him every week. He's starting to get pretty real about his fears about his history and this weekend he started to talk about some pretty inappropriate stuff with his older brother. I feel like we're getting to the heart of his relapse stuff."

"Sounds like you're doing some good work," says Janet, who is currently supervising him as an Intern.

"Sounds like he's going to need a referral," adds Kym.

"Oh, for sure. But toward the end of my shift yesterday I noticed that his chores weren't being done, and it looks like he hasn't washed his sheets and towels for a while. Normally, as the CD Tech, I would call this to his attention and enforce the rules. But it felt weird, like I was afraid he would take it personally, you know?"

"So what did you do?" asks the Clinical Director.

"Honestly, I didn't do anything. I felt stuck, and decided to talk about it with you guys today since it wasn't urgent."

"I can see the dilemma, man," says Ricardo who avoids conflict like the plague on general principle. "You were afraid it would mess up your counseling relationship."

"Exactly. We have been talking about such personal issues, that jamming him up about his sheets seemed petty to me."

The Clinical Director sat forward, looking irritable. "It depends on whether or not you see the value of the structure. Do you believe the structure is therapeutic?" he asks.

Jesse ponders this. "They need external structure because their internal world is so chaotic. Yeah, they need it. I see what you mean."

"I think you are getting stuck in the "jammed up" thing," Janet offers. "You aren't jamming them up when you call attention to the structure, you're teaching them to be accountable for their self-care. Maybe we can talk more about this in supervision later," she suggests, and Jesse nods in relief.

"What's the scoop with the new admit, Brian?" the Clinical Director asks as he reads the log.

"I was looking at the intake and it says he is 25 years old, dropped out of college and is living with his folks. They are worried because he is drinking daily in his room and doesn't seem to eat. He spends most of his time fighting on the phone with his girlfriend who apparently uses methamphetamine. They brought him to treatment as an ultimatum – clean up or move. He elected to enter treatment."

"All he did this weekend was sleep and eat a lot," Jesse offers. "He did go to the outside meeting with us but went straight to bed when we got home."

"That sounds more like a cocaine or meth detox than an alcoholic," observes Sarah.

"Yeah, it does," says Janet. "I'm guessing there's more to be revealed."

"It's possible Mom and Dad really don't know what's going on. They see the alcohol bottles and make assumptions. Is the meth girlfriend going to be joining the parents for Family day?" Kym asks with a smile.

"Well, that would be fun!" Janet grins. "I'll meet with him later and get a feel for him and his support system. I'll be clear with him that we can UA anyone who enters the building so if she does come, and if she looks loaded, we can test her. Sarah, are you on shift Saturday?

"Yes I am. I'll have a cup ready," she smiles.

"The young girl, Cathy, is going to be a handful," says Eddie. "I've only had her for two groups, and I got enough attitude for the week!"

"Yes, I had my own dose of F.U. from Ms. Cathy this morning," says Janet.

"I kind of like her," says Sarah. "She's just being real. She obviously thinks being here is bullshit, and she's not pretending. I prefer her to the guys who just comply with everything and have no intention of getting clean."

"You mean like Tony?" says Jorge. "That dude is gaming every time he opens his mouth!"

"Yeah, he is," says Ricardo. "And I'm worried because he is coming up for graduation pretty soon, and I don't see any progress. I'm wondering if we should hold him over, or let him loose and see what he does?"

"What would you want to see him do if you kept him?" asks the Clinical Director.

"Hmmm. I would want him to at least consider a connection between his using and work problems. Honestly, I don't think the guy sees it – he really thinks it's his boss and co-workers. He's damned lucky their HR department valued him enough to send him here, and I'm afraid they wasted their money."

"Well this hits close to home," says Eddie. "You guys cared enough about me to get me some help, and I was willing to take it. But without the willingness, I'm not sure anything is gonna change, bro," he says to Ricardo.

"Have you talked about your concerns to Tony directly?" asks Janet. "Maybe you could lay it out to him straight, like you are giving it to us, and see if that gets in. It's worth a shot. If he still doesn't hear it, he's making your decision for you, and we let him complete," she suggests.

"I like it," says the Clinical Director as he shuts the log.

"We're not supposed to work harder on their recovery than they are, right Janet?" Keisha smiles.

"Anything you want to add from Family day last week?" the Clinical Director asks Kym

"I met with Jeff and his wife, who seem to be making progress with their communication. She did a good job addressing her concerns about his depression, and she was encouraging him to take the medication even though it makes him kinda sleepy the first couple of weeks. She really sees the connection between his mood and his drinking. After listening to you, Jesse, it looks like there may be some trauma that goes along with his depression. Maybe even a molestation he'll have to work through."

"No wonder he keeps relapsing. That's a lot to carry," says Jorge.

Jorge

Jorge would know. He was sexually molested by his older cousin for two years, between 6 and 8 years old, when his cousin lived with the family. Jorge never told anyone about this, deeply ashamed that somehow it was his fault and he would get in trouble because he knew it was "wrong." Jorge started smoking weed as soon as it became available to him, and he remained loaded on one chemical or another for years. He did his steps 3 times before he finally had a sponsor he was willing to tell about it, and his sponsor recommended that he talk to a counselor. It took him another year before he saw the counselor. He would not have done so, but he was going to be having surgery, and recognized that he was already fantasizing about getting extra narcotics the "legit" way. He did not want to lose his 7 years of recovery, so told on himself to his sponsor, and agreed the call the counselor the next day. He has been in counseling for a year now, and while he still is deeply private about his past, he no longer feels responsible. It was as though a weight had been lifted off of him, and coincidentally, he has lost 30 pounds in the process. He could finally feel safe enough to stop hiding his body.

"I also met with Cathy's parents, who are really frustrated. They don't get the disease thing at all, and are wondering if she should go to one of those wilderness programs for young adults from here to 'get her shit together' says her father," Kym adds.

"Why did she agree to come?" asks Sarah.

"She was told she would have to go live with her grandparents in Iowa if she didn't get clean and sober and go to school. Apparently that's a WORSE threat than a month in treatment, so this is the lesser of the evils I think. "

"It's interesting that all of their solutions seem to involve getting rid of her, abandoning her. I wonder if that's a common parenting threat for her – do it or else you will go away," Janet wonders.

"Well, if that's true, then substances may BE her secure attachment," Kym agrees. "That's going to make it really hard for her to let go. She trusts the substances – she's not so sure about the adults."

"No wonder I like her," Sarah laughs. "I get the abandonment thing."

"Well, I don't know as much about the attachment thing, like you `learned' women, but I do know an addict when I see her. I really would like to interrupt her cycle before she makes a career out of it," says the Clinical Director.

Janet looks up at the clock and slips out for Process Group.

Process Group

Janet watched the group trail in and take the seats they have chosen as "their seat." Since Brian was new, he was going to have to negotiate his way through the hierarchy to see where he would land. As she watches this, Janet thinks of a National Geographic tape she shows about stress that features work with baboons, and how their place in the hierarchy affects their stress levels. Brian appears to need to sit by her, which is his way to establish his presence. In fact, she notices that Brian appears to need to be seen, which is going to be a challenge. It could be helpful if it's anxiety based, and it could create tension as he vies for Alpha position with her. *"I always win,"* she reminds to herself.

"Good afternoon, guys. I was thinking about Community group this morning, and about Keisha spending too much energy trying to get you where you need to be. In thinking about it I

The Work Goes On

probably should have handled it differently. However, it strikes me that a lot of us get caught up in doing too much for other people, over-giving, and it can cause a lot of resentment, and even drug use. Can anyone but me relate to this?" she says with a smile.

Donna's hand shoots up. "I do this all the time. I was raised in the South, and southern women get value by being 'nice,' or being helpful. When I would leave the house my mamma would say, "Now honey, you be good. Be nice." I really don't know sometimes when I am being nice and when I am overdoing it. But I sure know when I get tired of doing it and get pissed off!" she laughs.

"So do we!" laughs Jeff. "You were snarky the other day during double scrub when I asked you to get us some more sponges," he reminds her.

Donna grins, "I was tired of being such a good sport."

"Do you think you drank as an excuse to stop being a good sport, or so that you could tolerate being a good sport?" Janet asked her.

Donna thought a minute. "I think both, really. It depends on the situation. If I'm honest, I think I used alcohol to give me permission to say things I was too afraid to say sober."

"I can so relate to that!" says Lonnie. "Only in my case, I just took more pills – 'my medicine.' Then when my husband would call me on something I said, I would blame it on the pills."

"I think I worry about being a 'bad guy'," Jeff adds. "I'm afraid I'm going to look like a selfish prick like my dad if I say 'no' or 'that won't work for me.'"

"Why are the only two choices nice or a prick?" Janet asks him.

Jeff looks at Tony and Jason. "Help me out here, guys. Is there another choice?" he asks.

"I think there's the option to be direct about our feelings without having to be a dick about it," Alan suggests. "But it feels weird."

The Work Goes On

"You did a great job this morning," says Janet. "So it's possible to do."

"I don't know about this," says Tony. "My boss is such an asswipe that I don't think direct would get through. Sometimes the only thing that works IS to be a prick," he offers.

"When you've faced him down like that, what has happened next?" asks Janet.

Tony thinks for a minute. "Nothing really. He goes back to his office."

"Does the thing you were arguing with him about change after you challenge him like that?"

"No, I guess not. Even if I get my way, he finds another way to get me later." Tony admits

"But if you don't say something they'll keep on punking you," Brian adds.

"Good point. So, not saying anything isn't going to work, and bullying isn't going to work. What else can you do?" Janet asks him.

"I guess I can think about what I want to say, and back it up with facts to argue my point instead of getting loud?" Tony asks.

"Have you ever tried that?" she asks.

He shakes his head no.

"Maybe you can role play in your one-on-one's with Ricardo and get some ideas about how you might want to carry yourself when you get back to work," Janet suggests.

"Can I practice how to talk to my Mom later?" Cathy asks.

Surprised, Janet says, "You sure can. That's what we're here for."

Cathy just nods and sits back.

The Work Goes On

Supervision

Jesse comes into the office in time for weekly supervision with Janet.

"I want to pick up on our conversation at Staffing this morning. I know the dual role thing is hard for you."

"Yeah, it is. I'm not always sure what part of me I'm using. It doesn't seem right to 'enforce' rules when I'm trying to create a therapeutic alliance."

"Actually, it's the therapeutic alliance that's the money in the bank when it comes time to set boundaries when we need to. It's the art of what we do. We have to find a way to maintain our connection, which usually means letting them know the purpose of the rules rather than just enforcing them. Is this a counter-transference issue in some way?"

"Well, I admit I hated the structure when I was a client, and I did think the counselors were on power trips when they would write me up," he smiles.

"I imagine you were a handful," Janet laughs. "So part of your transition as a professional is to see yourself as a counselor and accept the authority that comes with it. They need us to be their external frontal lobe, remember? Their judgment isn't fully on board and their self-neglect runs deep. I think that's true for most recovering people, no matter how much clean time we put together. I have 26 years and I am STILL learning this," Janet smiles ruefully.

Now tell me where you're going with Jeff, and what you're thinking about referral," Janet suggests.

As supervision is wrapping up Eddie is returning for his evening shift.

Eddie

Eddie was out on medical leave after taking a few client medications over a year ago. Since his return he no longer handles the medication, and he is doing a much better job with client engagement and management. He told Janet in confidence that the Clinical Director suggested he get a depression evaluation, and he did. He also got a physical and discovered he had Hep C which explained symptoms like fatigue, difficulty reading, and mood swings. He went on a 6 month course of interferon which seems to have put his Hep C in remission. Eddie's marriage has survived that rocky period, and he is back on track with his NA program. He has agreed to continue working with his sponsor and meetings as a condition of return to work. He is now the agency's lead cheer-leader for self-care!

"Hey, Eddie. How was your afternoon?" Jesse asks as he is putting on his riding gear.

"I was walkin' the walk, man! Coffee with my sponsor, a little nap, I am ready to rock and roll," he grins.

Janet looks at the clock and needs to leave for her own therapy appointment.

"Guys, I am out of here. Eddie, you're the man!" Janet throws over her shoulder as she takes off.

Janet

"Something weird happened today, and I want to check my part of it," Janet tells her therapist.

Her therapist cocks her head.

"I fronted off Keisha in front of community group about her codependent behavior, and later she confronted me about it, and I made amends."

"So, what's the problem?"

"Earlier that morning I had been watching her with the clients, and was thinking how graceful she is, how well she carries herself, and frankly how beautiful she is."

"You wonder if these are connected."

"I don't think so at a conscious level, but I've been thinking about our last session, when I said I was afraid of bimbos."

"You said you were afraid to compete with bimbos," the therapist adds.

"Yeah. I wonder if I was feeling jealous or threatened by her so I made her look bad."

"You were competing with her or she was competing with you?" the therapist clarifies

"Oh, it's definitely me. And she's not a bimbo at all. But she's younger, beautiful, and has so much of her life ahead of her. Honestly, I look like her frumpy Aunt. Maybe I was trying to maintain my value by looking smarter than her."

"If you don't like being frumpy, you could change it," the therapist points out.

"I know. I just don't feel like making the effort. Maybe it's the avoiding intimacy thing again. Nothing says 'I'm not available' like cruller crumbs down your shirt!" Janet giggles. "Waking up drenched from night sweats isn't helping. Neither are my new "progressive lenses," which is another word for 'bifocals'," she smiles.

Her therapist smiles. "Just because you practice self-care doesn't mean you have to jump into intimacy, you know. It's a process you get to control."

Janet just sighs.

As she heads home she decides NOT to get the frozen yogurt after all, and has a bowl of watermelon.

TUESDAY

The Department of Corrections van is pulling away as Janet arrives on Tuesday morning, indicating that the latest state release client has been delivered. No doubt Jorge is getting him squared away, and Janet feels a sigh of relief that she will be meeting with Brian instead. Her attitude troubles her, because Janet has always prided herself in her ability to work with the unworkable. *"What is it about prison culture that is so hard for me?"* she asks herself.

She starts thinking back to a workshop she attended on the Culture of Incarceration, and what she learned about the convict code:

- Inmates should mind their own affairs.
- Inmates should not inform the staff about the illicit activities of other prisoners.
- Inmates should be indifferent to staff.
- Conning and manipulation skills are valued

As she thought about it more, it was the over-controlled emotion, the "face" that institutionalized people often wear that makes them hard to read and understand. They've learned to "get over" as a way of asserting power indirectly because direct power isn't available to them. There's a learned indifference, a distancing that's required, even if it's feigned, that makes their attempts to be friendly or cooperative look suspicious. There's always a game, and if she's honest with herself, she knows she's been "had" more than once. She isn't willing to be paranoid enough to stay as alert as she would need to be to catch it every time. It's so much work to monitor boundaries all the time, to have someone pushing against her or manipulating around them.

When she's completely honest, rigorously honest, she's triggered by their willingness to bully and intimidate while claiming to be victims themselves. Even when they admit they have harmed someone it is still caused by their own victimization first. *"They always feel like they have something coming,"* she thinks.

"Then again, when I think about my outrage at David and the bimbo aren't I saying the same thing? I had a right to send him emotionally abusive emails because he hurt me first!" Janet smiles to herself as she remembers her sponsor calling 'bullshit" on this logic and she had to take responsibility for her responses regardless of provocation.

"Maybe I'm just jealous that they get to keep their denial while I have to own my shit!" she grins to herself as she opens the door to the office. Ricardo glances up and grins back at her and returns to his intake with the new admit, J.P.

J.P is a 34 year old Caucasian male, recently released after serving a year for a parole violation. He is a chronic offender, possession, sales and distribution, who has previously attempted addiction treatment. He has managed to avoid state time for the most part because his wealthy grandmother continues to give him access to a trust fund left by his grandfather so he always has private legal representation. His grandmother paid for his last treatment episode as well as this one, so he is private pay versus parole funded. In his mind, that makes him "self-referred" which translates into entitled. Ricardo is going to have his work cut out for him.

Janet feels herself being checked out, then dismissed by the younger man, which irritates her right away. Fortunately, she is meeting with the new client, Brian, so she takes her coffee and the log with her to another room to review, and then goes to get Brian from the yoga class.

As Brain settles himself into a chair across from her, Janet takes a moment to eyeball him even though he was in her process group the day before.

Brian

"Good morning, Brian," Janet smiles. "I know we met briefly at group yesterday, so I am glad I can spend some one-on-one time with you today. First I want to get to know your story a little and then we are going to go through an ASAM assessment, which is a psychosocial interview. Our job is to figure out what kind of treatment plan is going to be best for you. This is your recovery – so it needs to be a treatment plan you choose. Do you have any questions?" Janet asks.

Brain nods no, so Janet continues.

She sits back in her chair and asks, "Why are you here? Why now?"

"My parents said they were going to throw me out if I didn't check in. Really, I think they put me in here to keep me away from my girlfriend, Brittany. They don't think she's good enough for me."

"It sounds like treatment really isn't your idea. Your parents seem to think alcohol and drug use is part of the problem even if they don't like Brittany."

"That's because I lost my job and have been missing classes, so I've been drinking more because I'm bored. There's nothing else to do but smoke some weed and play video games until I pick Brittany up after work."

"Why do you pick Brittany up?"

"Because she got this bullshit DUI, and doesn't have a license. I think the cop was just looking for an excuse to pull her over because she's hot. She blew a .09 and wasn't even drunk!"

"What happened to your job?" Janet asks.

"I'm not sure. I was working at Longs and after the holidays I was getting fewer and fewer hours until they stopped calling me completely. It's okay though, my boss was a jerk so it was probably just as well."

"And school?" she asks.

"I missed the first week of school because the school didn't tell me I could walk in and add, so I couldn't get into all the classes I needed. I wound up with bogus classes first thing in the morning, and I'm not a morning kind of guy, you know? It didn't work for me."

"You know Brian, you're 25 so you don't really have to be here. I'm wondering if there is something in your life YOU worry about, something in your life YOU would like to change? You seem like you're way too bright to spend your time watching Gilligan's Island and toking up all day so you can chauffeur your girlfriend to DUI class."

Brian grins at her.

Janet sits forward, "It seems to me that you've been on the drift plan. Is there something else you want in your life, Brian, or is this it?" Janet wonders.

"Uh, I really am pretty bored. The only thing I have to look forward to is Brittany, and we've been fighting a lot lately."

"Do you fight more when you party together?"

"Well, I get kind of jealous after I've done a couple lines. She says I get controlling."

"So you are either controlling or passive, is that it?" she clarifies.

"I guess so," he agrees.

"So that's why you encouraged Tony to speak up yesterday in process group. You were relating to him," she points out.

Brian smiles, pleased that she remembered.

"Okay, let's run through this assessment so I can get more details about your using history, your emotional life, work life, etc. We'll figure something out from there, okay?" Janet proposes.

Janet wraps up her interview too late to join Community group, so takes the chance to check and return phone calls and type up her assessment with Brian. As she is finishing, Ricardo and Jorge enter the office.

"Ricardo! I saw your new guy when I got here. What's the

The Work Goes On

poop?" Janet asks.

Ricardo and Jorge look at each other and sigh.

"Oh, dear," Janet laughs.

"So homeboy is a wanna be. He thinks he's a badass but hides behind grandma's skirts. There's a serious disconnect between who he is and who he THINKS he is." Ricardo says.

"What he IS is entitled," says Jorge. "Dude is already complaining about the lack of closet space. He's worried about where he is going to keep his 'equipment' he's asking his grandma to bring for Family day."

"What kind of equipment is he talking about?" Janet asks.

"He needs his special work out gear so he can get 'ripped'. They took the weights out the prison, so he lost some of his 'form'. He needs space for his supplements and shakes so he can 'bulk up' baby!" Ricardo laughs.

Janet giggles. "Apparently he thinks he has arrived at Promises in Malibu!"

"Girlfriend, if this was Promises, they would already HAVE all that shit! No, dude will be slumming with us," Ricardo says.

"So what did you tell him?" she asks Jorge.

"I told him, "This is all the space there is, Bro. You gonna have to make do. And don't have your grandma bring anything until you run it by Ricardo. Otherwise, that shit will just stay in her car."

"Oh, Ricardo. He bounced him back to you. Your favorite – saying "no"!" Janet teases.

"I hate this shit, man. Why can't they just do the deal? Why do we have to have these kinds of issues?"

"That's like asking, 'Why don't they just grow up?' Oh, that's right. Their frontal lobe isn't working very well. They're really 16 years old," she laughs.

"I'll deal with it during his assessment later," Ricardo says reluctantly.

"I'm going to do Psycho-ed group right now, so I'll leave you to it," Janet says as she grabs her curriculum binder and heads toward the squeaking, shuffling chairs in the group room.

Psychoeducation

"Good morning, guys. I thought we would spend some time today talking about Attitudes about Drinking and Use. There's no right or wrong here, I'm just taking a look at some common thoughts people have and then we'll discuss them. Look at your handout, and I'll give you a minute to fill it out.

While they were filling out their sheets, Janet hoped that this non-judgmental approach to the discussion would encourage clients like Brian and Tony, who are in precontemplation (don't see substances as a problem) to at least consider the possibility that alcohol use plays a role in their lives. Sometimes moving from precontemplation to contemplation (weighing the pros and cons of using) might be the best outcome we could expect in 30 days of treatment.

CHOOSE FOUR OF THESE WHICH ARE CLOSEST TO YOUR FEELINGS ABOUT ALCOHOL AND DRUG USE.

__ Should be accepted as normal behavior

__ Can cause some people great problems

__ Is good and beneficial

__ Should be feared by all

__ Can help some people relax and feel better

__ Is an individual decision

__ Should be presented honestly and objectively in school

__ Can relieve tensions

__ Is an "evil" which should be stressed in schools

___ Is acceptable, appropriate behavior by most

___ Creates problems for all young people

___ Is learned behavior

___ Is appropriate behavior by teenagers

___ Encourages individuals to solve problems artificially

___ Is an escape from reality

Predictably the list encourages a lot of back and forth debate, which includes some silliness, as clients were able to be honest about their feelings about using. It's important that they get to tell the truth even if it's not what the counselor wants to hear!

After group Janet heads back to the office to chart the session, and passes an irritated looking J.P. leaving his meeting with Ricardo.

"Well, by the look on J.P's face it looks like you set a limit big guy!" Janet teased.

Ricardo looks tired and covers his face with his hands. "He feels like this place should be about health, and that preventing him from his equipment is like denying him physical therapy. Lord, have mercy." Ricardo says into his hands.

"Playing peek-a-boo with me isn't going to change it," Janet laughs.

Ricardo peeks at her through his fingers. "I'd rather look at you, trust me. Thank God I have my own sponsor. I can see a fourth step over this guy in my horizon," he says.

"Let me treat us both to a little Taco Bell. Should I get your usual?" Janet offers.

Ricardo smiles at her. "Gracias, my friend. I think I'll hide in Facebook – fake life- for a few minutes."

"I'll be right back" she says over her shoulder.

Process Group

Janet watches the group get settled in their chairs, and opens the group for check-in. As the clients are going around the room she notices J.P pouting, and notices Cathy watching him pout. She looks like she's evaluating him, which is interesting.

"I need to check in," says Tony. "I feel like I'm supposed to 'admit' that I'm an alcoholic when I don't really believe that."

"What's creating the pressure for you?" asks Janet.

"Well the groups, like the one this morning, keep focusing on how our alcohol and drug use has affected our life, reasons we drink and use, etc., and I see stress as my primary problem. If my boss wasn't a prick I wouldn't drink so much. I think my boss sent me to H.R. for treatment so he could blame me instead of his bad management."

"I think a lot of people struggle with stress, Tony, and most of us don't have a lot of skills to deal with it. So we start to use the same solution over and over. Sometimes what starts out as a solution to a problem or a stress reliever becomes the problem or stressor. It can sneak up on you like that. Can anyone else relate to Tony's feelings?" she asked the group.

"I can," says Jeff. "I thought if my wife would stop nagging me and I had more energy I wouldn't relapse. I blamed her a lot. I even thought about divorcing her to cure my drinking!" he laughs. "It wouldn't have worked, but it seemed reasonable at the time," Jeff adds.

"But, see, I don't think I have an addiction to relapse to. Yeah, I went a little overboard at the Christmas party, and I may have been a little less sharp after a three day weekend every now and then, but I still have a job. I still go to work every day. My Dad was what you guys would say is a 'real' alcoholic. He would lose his jobs, fall down, make my mom cry. I'm nothing like that!" Tony emphasizes.

"I can see where you're coming from," says Donna. "My mom drank every day, and I didn't. I could go a whole month or two without a drink. The problem is that once I started drinking I couldn't stop. I wouldn't stop. Then my binges started getting closer together which was affecting my energy, so I started using cocaine to give me the picker up I needed. Then I figured out I could drink more when I used cocaine because I didn't get tired. Dude, it was all bad eventually."

Janet turned to Tony. "Tony, you mentioned your father's drinking, and how it affected the family. What would it mean about YOU if you were also an alcoholic?" Janet asks.

"You mean if I were like him?" Tony says.

Janet nods.

"Then I would be an irresponsible shit head; a failure" he says heatedly.

"So, if you admit that your drinking is a problem, you would be a failure as a man and a human being?" she asked gently.

Tony started to tear up, then pushes it away. "Maybe," he says.

"I can relate," says Alan. "I've been afraid of being my dad my whole life. And here I am in rehab. As I was listening to Tony I realized that's a major reason I fought coming to treatment. I couldn't admit that I failed."

Tony smiles at him slightly.

Janet looks at the group. "You guys are doing some really powerful work right now. This is what group is all about," she smiles. "Who else wants to jump in?" she asks.

After group Janet has scheduled a brief check-in with the Clinical Director since she's the lead counselor. He's not present for the day-to-day operations, but wants to feel 'in the loop' and she doesn't blame him. What is less predictable is his mood, which can range from angry to irritable to intolerant to calm in a brief period of time. She sees his car outside so knows he has already arrived and is probably looking through the log book.

Sure enough, his reading glasses are perched on his nose as she enters the office. "Greetings, chief," she says with a smile as she puts her charts down.

"Hi there," he answers still reading. Then he looks up.

"So, this new guy, J.P, looks like a piece of work. He wants to bulk up?" he asks with irritation.

Janet smiles. "So it appears."

"It really pisses me off when these guys get a chance to do a program instead of sit their happy asses in jail and instead of having a little gratitude they bitch about what they think they SHOULD be getting," he says.

Janet is never surprised when he is pissed off. "Well, Ricardo and Jorge handled it pretty well. The little guy is pouting right now, but they set the standard." Janet says.

"I worry about Ricardo and setting limits. The guy worries too much about being liked. I never worried about that shit – I was worried about doing the next right thing," he points out. Of course, as a Synanon graduate from the 70's, he is a product of confrontation counseling so emphasizing client engagement still seems like enabling to him.

"Is the new guy, Brian, settling in?" he asks.

"He's really on the drift plan," she says. "We're going to have to work on developing a self so he can feel connected to whatever choices HE makes. It makes me wonder about his parents and if they may have been hovering too much. He doesn't seem to have an inner compass."

"Well you're good at that guidance stuff, Janet," the Clinical Director says. "You'll figure it out,"

"That's what I told him," she smiles.

"I've been thinking about letting Sarah work some of the night shifts with Eddie now that she has finished school. Being a CD tech doesn't really use all her skills, and we could use a per diem counselor when you guys go on vacation," the Clinical Director suggests.

"Vacation?" Janet asks with pretend confusion.

"Yeah, that time when you aren't here and supposedly taking care of   yourself," he laughs.

"Oh, that. That would imply a personal life." Janet says. "I think that's a great idea, and I am sure she would be thrilled." Janet agrees.

The Clinical Director smiles. "Since I have your blessing I'll give her a call."

"I think you should talk to Eddie about it though. He may feel like you are putting her in there to keep an eye on him because he relapsed," Janet suggests.

"That's not it!" he says irritably. "I just want her to keep her skills up until we grow enough to create a counselor position for her."

"I know that. I also know this could be sensitive for him, and if he gets paranoid about her taking his job it could get really unpleasant between them. I think it's better to head it off at the pass," she continues.

"Okay, I take your point. You're always breaking out the baby powder! I'll talk to him when he gets here for his shift in a few minutes. Speaking of which, shouldn't you be clocking out?" he asks.

Janet nods. "Yep, I have a 6:00 women's meeting and I want to grab something to eat on the way. See you later," she calls as she bustles out the door.

WEDNESDAY

Janet arrives as Carl is leaving the next morning. He's late to leave because he decided to have breakfast with the clients, a perk of his job.

"Hey girl," Carl greets her and gives her a fist bump. "All is pretty peaceful. The egg timers you got for the showers seem to be helping. Shower times seem to be smoother," he comments.

"Hey there yourself. Glad to hear the hygiene is happening!" she smiles. "How are you, anyway? I don't run into you very often," she asks.

"I'm blessed, sister, blessed," he smiles. "I'm wondering if I still have enough brain cells to go to school. I was talkin' to Keisha, and it would be cool to go class with someone I know. School wasn't so good for me when I was younger and I'm man enough to admit it scares me a little."

"I think you could take one class and check out the brain cell situation for yourself," Janet suggests. "Besides, you work the perfect shift for a student. It allows you to study."

"Instead of jack off at my computer" she thinks as she remembers the computer virus from his evening porn adventures last year.

Carl nods. "Besides, Keisha's smarter than I am, so maybe she can tutor me!" he laughs. This statement gives Janet pause and she makes a mental note to watch for Keisha's exploitation in the future. Then she hears her sponsor saying, *"And this is your business, how?"*

Carl has done a good job staying off the porn sites at work once he was caught. It was particularly embarrassing because he maintains his sobriety through church participation. He's wondered why the guys he knows at church seem to have a tough time with porn – maybe it has something to do with repressing so many of their wants and needs. They have to leak out somehow! Carl has instead become addicted to Candy Crush on his phone, and Angry Birds on Facebook.

They are distracting and keep him awake, and don't threaten his job. Challenging himself by learning something new would be good for him, but he worries about his dyslexia. It's a source of shame for him.

Janet smiles at him. "I say, go for it. Your mind stays young when you use it, Dude."

Carl laughs as he walks out to his car.

Ricardo passes Carl coming in, his usual 15 minutes late. "Hey, Janet. How's it going?"

"Ricardo, my man. All is well in my world. Then again, I haven't looked in the log book yet, so more is to be revealed," she says.

"Tell me the highlights," he asks as he starts to check his voicemail.

"Hmmmmm. It says here that J.P was pushing Eddie pretty hard last night to let him use the phone even though he's on phone restriction the first week. He wanted to leave a message for his lawyer. And I quote, "Even when I get popped I get to make a phone call." Janet laughs.

Eddie grimaces. "Did he make the call?" he asks with the phone cradled on his shoulder.

"No, Eddie held firm and told him to take it up with you this morning."

"Oh, shit."

They are interrupted by a quick knock and in walks J.P. himself.

"Bro, I need to use the phone to call my lawyer," J.P. insists.

"Okay. What's going on?" Ricardo asks.

"It's Nonya," J.P. answers.

"What's that?"

"None of your business, man. It's between me and my lawyer."

Ricardo rolled his eyes before he could stop himself, which

aggravated J.P further.

"Don't give me any shit, man. I'm not a prisoner here. I have rights."

"Actually, you are a prisoner here, J.P. Your acceptance is considered custodial, which means you still belong to the Department of Corrections until you successfully complete this program. Your options are to complete this program, and its requirements, or to return to institutional custody. Should I call your parole officer right now, since I'm already on the phone?" Ricardo asks.

J.P. and Janet just stare at Ricardo. "Dude, back up. There's no need to roll me up. I just want to speak to my attorney about a couple of things, including my right to have my equipment here." J.P. offers.

"That would be no problem, J.P. The deal is you need to talk to staff with respect or you don't get jack, do you get it?"

J.P. nods.

"When I am done checking my messages I'll let you know and you can call your attorney."

Janet is still staring at Ricardo as J.P. leaves the room. "WOW! Someone's been watching Law and Order! Ricardo you were splendid. I am so proud of you."

Ricardo grinned. "Something in me snapped. I guess he's such a punk I don't give a shit if he likes me. That was kind of fun," he admits.

"Maybe you should teach the boundary lecture," Janet suggests with a smile.

Ricardo finishes his calls and goes out to call J.P to use the phone. J.P. saunters in, and dials. "Hey, John, this is J.P. I need some legal advice, man. Give me a call here at the treatment center when you can, okay?" and he hangs up.

The Work Goes On

Community Group

Janet, Ricardo, and J.P. join Jorge for Community meeting which is uneventful except for an exchange between J.P. and Cathy.

"I know you just got here and all, but I think you should put away your bowl after breakfast instead of leave it for someone else to pick up," Cathy begins.

J.P. looks up and away from her without acknowledging that she spoke.

"Seriously, dude, I don't want to clean up after you. I'm on breakfast chore, so I have to make sure everything is done or I get marked down."

J.P. looks at her. "Whatever."

Janet interrupts this exchange. "J.P., there's a certain respect we have to show each other for treatment to be a safe place. I get it you've been operating in a very different environment, and your style probably works for you there. But here, we have a different culture. Could you answer Cathy again with more respect?" she requests. As she is asking this, she is smiling inside because Cathy spoke to her in exactly the same way on Monday, so turnabout is fair play!

"Okay, okay," J.P. says as he looks at Cathy. "I will wash my own bowl."

"Thank you," Cathy says with a smile.

The group takes a small break before Ricardo's psycho-education class, which allows Janet to suggest a one-on-one with Donna to follow-up on Monday's women's group.

As Ricardo begins his opening warm-up, Janet can hear him speak with a little more authority. "Facing down J.P did him some good," Janet thinks. Soon Donna comes in and takes a seat.

Donna

"Hey, Donna. I've been thinking about that statement you made in women's group, "I drink the poison hoping they will die," which is something my sponsor has said to me. You obviously have had some clean time before," Janet observes.

"Well, this isn't my first rodeo for sure. I've been trying to beat this thing on and off for ten years."

"What's your longest period of sobriety?"

"I had three years before my last relapse."

"What do you think took you out?" Janet wonders.

"I was in my first sober relationship with a woman I thought I would spend the rest of my life with. When I look at it now, I was scared to death. So I started picking on her, being critical, and finally blamed her when I started drinking. I just don't think I could handle being that close to someone."

Janet was relating. "So, do you think you weren't ready for the intimacy maybe?"

"Oh, I'm sure. I got all kinds of paranoid thoughts that she was trying to control me, trying to smother me, trying to take away all my freedom. You know they say lesbians date with a U-Haul!"

Janet laughs. "I've heard that."

"Well in my case it was true. I thought that when someone wanted me as much as I wanted them it would be enough. So I dove right in and started to get weird. I didn't know how to get space without creating a fight. I just didn't have the tools. At the same time, pushing her away was killing me because I loved her, so I started to drink to make it easier."

"And did it?"

"What, make it easier?"

"Uh, huh."

"Yes and no. I mean it made it easier to separate because I was numb. But I have so many regrets, so many things I wish I hadn't said or done. I did some terrible damage to that woman, and I feel so ashamed," she says as tears begin to roll down her cheeks.

The Work Goes On

"Have you talked to her since you've been here?" Janet asks.

"Oh, no. She left my f**ked up ass 6 months ago, and rightly so. The ship was going down and I would have taken her with me. I WAS taking her with me," she says as she sniffles.

"So, it sounds like your issues are mostly Al-anon and Codependency issues," Janet observes.

"I thought Codependents were clingy – I pushed her away."

"I know. Codependency is really about the behaviors we do because we don't trust our attachments to other people. We're always waiting for the shoe to drop and they'll leave. Some codependents handle this by being anxious and clingy, and some deal with it by trying not to fully attach to start with so we don't get hurt when they leave. It sounds like you're the pushing away kind," Janet explains.

"How did I get like this?"

"Well. I suspect it has something to do with your alcoholic Mom who wasn't there for you, so you learned to depend only on yourself pretty young. Trusting other people may be really hard for you, and really scary."

"So, I'm not going to fix this in 30 days, huh?" jokes Donna.

"No, ma'am," Janet laughs with her "This one takes a while, and can't heal unless you're sober. We need to hook you up with a Codependency therapist, and you'll need to add an Al-anon program to your AA."

"I've heard that Al-anon is graduate school for AA!" Donna smiles.

"I think that's true," Janet agrees.

Janet finishes her session with Donna and calls her own sponsor.

"Hi there. So, I just got done talking to someone about Al-non for her Codependency issues. You really think I should work another program? Get an Al-anon sponsor?" Janet asks.

The Work Goes On

"Why did you recommend it to the other woman?" her sponsor asks.

"Because she relapses around relationship stuff, attachment stuff like I'm working on with my therapist"

"So, you aren't relapsing. Why is it still a good idea?" she prompts.

Janet sighs. "Because other than you, I don't trust anyone but me. Sometimes I don't even trust us!" she laughs.

"So, it sounds like you may need to take your own advice, huh?"

"Actually it was YOUR advice, I just passed it on," Janet said.

"It's still valid. You have my support, honey. You have nothing to lose."

"You're right. I'll go tonight, I have a meeting list I've been carrying around in my purse for 6 months."

"Give me a call afterwards and tell me how you did," her sponsor suggests.

Ricardo enters the office as Janet is hanging up the phone. "That was fun," he says.

"What was your favorite part," Janet asks.

"The part where I got to talk about how fighting acceptance lead us to   resentments. I was able to share my own struggle with this and how my sponsor helped me with it," he says, putting his curriculum away.

Fortunately he's not looking at Janet who wants to roll her eyes. Ricardo still over-shares with the clients, convinced that they will identify with him and feel hopeful. This is the role of a sponsor, not a therapist. She wonders if it's because after four years as a counselor he still doesn't fully trust his clinical skills, so he keeps falling back on his own story to have "credibility" with the clients.

This is a common clinical mistake counselors make, and it's one of the counseling behaviors that make chemical dependency counselors seem less credible to other types of clinicians. It's not that you should NEVER share, but it should be done sparingly, only when it serves the client... and keep it to a sentence. Every time you are talking the client is not talking. It is their treatment, not the counselors'.

Janet decides to change the subject. "Ricardo, I was meeting with Donna, and I figured out that she really needs a codependency/Al-anon treatment plan. She's had chunks of sobriety before – it's her relationships that take her out."

Ricardo nods. "That makes sense. You can tell she's been around by the language she uses."

Janet quips "This isn't my first rodeo, she says! "

Ricardo smiles. "Sounds like it went well with her."

Janet smiles at him.

"It's lunch time. You fly, I'll buy!" Janet laughs. Ricardo heads out to Wendy's this time.

Process Group

Janet looks around the unusually quiet group pondering their silence. "Okay, I give. Will anyone tell me what's going on right now?" she asks.

Jason shifts in his chair. "Something happened at lunch."

"And . . ." Janet prompts.

"Well, someone has a cell phone and several of us have been using it."

"Oh, okay. This isn't a crisis, it's a rule violation. We can deal with this." Janet points out.

There is a collective change of energy as the secret is let out.

"So, how do you think we should deal with this?" Janet asks.

The Work Goes On

"I think the snitch should shut the hell up!" offers J.P.

"Well, I get the feeling that Alan is speaking for the group because it takes a lot of energy to keep a secret. A lot of you probably grew up with secrets, and they can really drain your energy," Janet replies to J.P.

"She's right," says Jeff. "I'm tired of it. It feels like High School."

"So, who has the phone?" Janet asks the group.

There's dead silence. "Okay, so you guys want the person to confess instead of throw them under the bus. Got it. Is it possible that this person is so used to keeping secrets in his/her addiction that they don't know how to tell on themselves? They've never done it, so expecting them to do it is unfair?"

The silence continues.

"Okay, we'll drop who for now. What's more interesting to me is how the secret has affected you. What's that been like?" Janet asks.

"I've had a really hard time with it,' Jason says. "That's why I had to say something. It brought up a lot of things for me. On the one hand, it was cool to feel included. I was nerdy in high school so I never got to be one of the cool kids. On the other hand, you guys are here to help us, and I felt like we were lying to you."

"I admit I've been distracted by it," says Tony. "I've tried not to get involved, but it's all the group seems to talk about. It's like the secret took over."

"What a great point,' Janet agreed. "It's like telling yourself, "Don't think about elephants, and don't think about elephants. All you can think about is elephants!"

"Exactly!" Tony agrees.

"It brought up for me how many secrets I kept from my husband. I think it's a form of control for me. I feel like I'm in control of something when I keep it a secret. It's weird that way," Lonnie says.

"I get that," Donna says. "I used to feel so out of control, powerless over myself, that a secret would make me feel like I had 'one up' on other people."

"You guys are making some really great points. Secrets can have a lot of power. So, my thought is that I'll ask you all to write a paragraph on the role of secrets in your addiction and give it to me tomorrow. In the meantime, I can have Jorge do a room search to locate the phone if the person doesn't surrender it after group. Does that make sense?" Janet asks.

"No," Cathy says. "Why should everyone have to write a paragraph when not everyone used the phone. That doesn't seem fair."

"You're writing because everyone kept a secret. It's not punishment, I think of it more like a journal exercise. Secrets are a big deal in recovery, they can make or break your sobriety. Your relapse will begin with secrets long before you take that first drink or drug. It's a serious warning sign, and if you have all been keeping a secret you've all been in relapse mode. I need to take this seriously and interrupt it quickly," Janet explains.

"I never thought about it as a relapse warning sign,' Donna said. "You're right. I was keeping secrets from my girlfriend way before I drank my first beer. Wow."

Janet smiles at her.

After process group, Janet heads to the office to log the paragraph assignment so Eddie can remind the clients after their group. She is about to go get Jorge when there is a knock and Brian enters the room.

Brian

"Okay, it was me. I had an extra phone stashed in the lining of my suitcase. I couldn't handle not talking to Brittany until Family day. I'm sorry I dragged the group into it," Brian says.

"What was so scary for you about being separated from Brittany, Brian?" Janet wonders.

"I don't know. It's just that I talk to her every day, and I worry about her when we don't text. I worry about what she's doing, and if she's okay."

"Why wouldn't she be okay?" Janet asks.

"I don't know. Sometimes she hangs around some sketchy people, and I worry that she might get taken advantage of. She can party pretty hard, and I feel better when I am there to look after her."

"Have you ever worried about yourself when you are hanging around these sketchy people?"

"Not really. I watch pretty carefully for the most part."

"Until you are wasted?"

"Well, yeah. I did have my wallet stolen once."

"So what do you imagine Brittany will do when she doesn't hear from you?"

"She'd get mad, worry that something bad happened."

"When she gets upset, what does she do?"

Brian thinks a minute. "She gets loaded."

"So, chances are when she doesn't hear from you she'll get loaded. Then what?"

"She'll eventually go home because she has to work tomorrow. The thing is, I am not sure how she's going to get home now that she doesn't have a car."

"Is this the part that worries you the most?"

"Yeah. Those guys can be real dogs."

"Okay, how about this. Why don't you text her that we caught you and you won't be able to talk to her until Family day. Remind her that she has to come to Family day straight - we test here. She may still drink after that, but you can let go of feeling like you abandoned her." Janet offers.

Brain grinned in relief. His fingers flew over the keys, and then he hands her back the phone. "That was cool of you, Janet."

"No problem. It was cool of you to turn yourself in. Not bad for only three days of recovery. We'll extend your phone time out by the three days you were hiding your cell, and I want you to write your paragraph like   everyone else. Okay?"

"Okay," he agrees, and heads off to his room.

Ricardo had been watching the exchange. "You know the Clinical Director would have been disappointed that he didn't get to do a room search, right?" he asks.

Janet laughs. "I know. He loves a good shake down. But I think this was better, don't you?" she asks.

"I think it was brilliant. He's really lost isn't he?"

"I get why his parents don't like the girlfriend. She sounds like a lot of work," says Janet.

"Poor kid. I remember being like that when I was using. I had a girlfriend who was a bigger addict than me, and spent half my time using to keep up with her. I suppose that's how my disease got really out of control now that I think about it," Ricardo says.

"Yeah. Relationships can kick your ass," nods Janet.

Janet thinks back to how much time and effort she spent trying to make David's life easier, and how she can see now it was also about control. Taking care of things made her indispensable in her own mind, and was supposed to protect her from the abandonment that inevitably came. It was as though her 'magic powers' of over-doing were going to keep the loss at bay. Her own life disappeared in the process, only to be left with neither her life nor his life when he took off with the bimbo. There was nothing but void.

Janet tries to shove these thoughts aside by spending the next hour or so charting, answering phone calls and then pulls out her Al-anon list. There's an Al-anon Adult Children of Alcoholics group at 6:00 near her house, so she heads on over. She feels silly that she's nervous, then cuts herself some slack that she'll be a newcomer in this fellowship.

There's less smoking outside the Al-non meeting than her AA meeting which makes her smile. However, the cookies and coffee are there, and she wanders over to the literature table noticing that they have different books and pamphlets than AA meetings. She grabs a Letting Go bookmark to read as she takes a seat so she will look like she's busy instead of just sitting there like a lump.

To let go does not mean to stop caring,
    it means I can't do it for someone else.

To let go is not to cut myself off,
    it's the realization I can't control another.

To let go is not to enable,
    but allow learning from natural consequences.

To let go is to admit powerlessness, which means
    the outcome is not in my hands.

To let go is not to try to change or blame another,
    it's to make the most of myself.

To let go is not to care for,
    but to care about.

To let go is not to fix,
    but to be supportive.

To let go is not to judge,
    but to allow another to be a human being.

To let go is not to be in the middle arranging all the outcomes,
    but to allow others to affect their destinies.

To let go is not to be protective,
    it's to permit another to face reality.

To let go is not to deny,
  but to accept.

To let go is not to nag, scold or argue,
  but instead to search out my own shortcomings and correct them.

To let go is not to adjust everything to my desires,
  but to take each day as it comes and cherish myself in it.

To let go is not to criticize or regulate anybody,
  but to try to become what I dream I can be.

To let go is not to regret the past,
  but to grow and live for the future.

To let go is to fear less and love more

Janet smiles at the language of the poem, and recognizes how many of the things she's supposed to let go of that she still holds on to. "God, I'll be here the rest of my natural life," she sighs.

Soon the meeting opens and she hears the familiar Twelve Steps and Traditions, and familiar discouraging of crosstalk, and she can feel herself calm down. She had expected a lot of complaining about alcoholics, but since this is an ACA meeting, a lot of people no longer live with active addiction. The focus is on how they're still acting in their adult lives in reaction to their childhood. "That would be me," she thinks. She is discovering a new set of "peeps" and she grins to herself in relief.

She looks forward to calling her sponsor when she gets home.

The Work Goes On

THURSDAY

Janet arrives at the same time as Ricardo which is, itself, a miracle. They fist bump in the driveway on the way in and are met at the office door by an exasperated Keisha.

"Thank God you're here. I swear I feel like I am herding cats!" she exclaims.

Janet and Ricardo put their coats on their chairs. "What's going on?" Ricardo asks.

"I've had a terrible time with that new guy, J.D.," she says.

"J.P.," Ricardo corrects.

"Whatever. I don't know what his problem is, but he refused to get up when the alarm went off, he took a 25 minute shower, and it's time for group and he's just now making his breakfast. It's like he's deliberately in a power struggle with me," she snaps.

"He probably is," Janet agreed. She looked at Ricardo, "What do you want to do? I have your back."

"What I want to do is bitch-slap him," Ricardo says with a frown. "You meant professionally, huh?"

Janet smiles. "I was heading there."

"What's really going on is a giant tantrum about his 'equipment.' Let's look in the log and see if his attorney called back. . . here it is. Yeah, and it looks like it was a really short conversation. His attorney probably blew him off."

"That would make sense. I can't imagine his attorney would spend time on crap like that," says Janet.

"So what he most wants is to have the rules not apply to him – to be special." Ricardo thinks out loud.

"So I think we should deny this request, and have him continue

The Work Goes On

his schedule with everyone else. You'll have him in your DBT group after Community meeting," Janet says. "Keisha and I will be doing Community with you, and I imagine the rest of the clients are getting tired of his shit," Janet continues.

"Maybe we can get them to give him some feedback about how he is affecting the rest of the house," she suggests.

Ricardo nods. "Okay. Let's go with that. Keisha, girl, I encourage you to take a minute and call someone who likes you and try to find a sense of humor. It really isn't personal. He's been this way most of his life, I would guess."

Keisha smiles at him and took her phone outside.

"Let's look at the rest of the log, and see what we see," Janet suggests

Carl notes that Brian slept badly, was up and down all night, *"Like he's jonesing,"* Janet thinks. Almost everyone worked on their secrets paragraphs for today, except Cathy and, of course, J.P. It surprises Janet for some reason that Cathy is not compliant, though she remembers that Cathy had been the one to object to the assignment yesterday. *"There's more to that girl. I think I'll call her in later this morning,"* Janet thinks.

Janet begins to check her voicemail as Ricardo heads out to lead the DBT group, and Jesse arrives for his Internship hours. He's curious about DBT and is delighted that he has a chance to learn.

Psychoeducation

Dialectical Behavior Therapy (DBT) is a form of psychotherapy that was originally developed by Marsha Linehan, Ph.D., to treat people with borderline personality disorder (BPD) and chronically suicidal individuals.

It's now used with a variety of populations including TBI, eating disorders, mood disorders, and chemical dependency. It combines standard cognitive behavior techniques for emotional regulation and reality testing with concepts of distress tolerance, acceptance, and mindful awareness largely developed from

Buddhist meditative practice. The groups in treatment are largely skill-based groups. Ricardo has received specialized training to provide DBT groups in chemical dependency treatment settings.

Ricardo encourages everyone to open their DBT workbooks to today's topic, Radical Acceptance.

Pain + Non-Acceptance = Suffering

It is easy to accept things you like. It is hard to accept things you hate, disapprove of, or that cause you a lot of pain. The higher the pain, the harder the acceptance. If you want things to change, accept them first, then change them. Reality is always changing and if you want to influence how it changes, you must first accept it.

Turning the Mind

What is Turning the Mind?

It is like walking down a road and coming to a fork where one road is accepting and one road is rejecting and choosing to turn toward the accepting road over and over again.

Steps to Turning the Mind

1. Notice…
   - anger, bitterness, annoyance, falling into the sea of "Why me?"
   - when you are trying to… escape reality, block things out, hide how you feel
2. Make an inner commitment to turn your mind toward acceptance
3. Practice turning your mind toward acceptance over and over again.

As Ricardo takes the clients through the worksheet, they discuss areas where they are struggling with Acceptance. 'Radical Acceptance" is a tough concept, and this takes up most of the group process. Brian is especially agitated, struggling with his inability to connect with Brittany and 'supervise' her. He is having trouble focusing, is anxious . . . he looks very much like a person in withdrawal, which Ricardo points out. Brian has never considered Brittany a drug, but everyone watching him is beginning to see it.

Ricardo works with Brian to practice Turning his Mind when he starts to have obsessive thoughts about Brittany, and the group recognizes how hard this is for him. Some of them recognize this struggle in their own lives, and are able to feel compassion for him. The session is going unusually well, and Jesse is thrilled with the model.

Cathy

Janet can hear the clients beginning to participate, as Cathy knocks on the door and comes in.

"Hey there, I wanted to touch base with you this morning. I noticed in the log that you didn't work on your paragraph last night, and I remembered that you didn't think it was fair yesterday. What's going on?"

Cathy's eyes were rings of coal this morning, the black eyeliner and black fingernails to match. However, her nails were chipped, which made her look very young. Janet could see how little she still is.

"I just thought it was lame, that's all. I think it's bogus punishing everyone for something only one person did."

"Is this fairness thing important to you?" Janet asks.

Cathy nods.

"Have you ever felt life wasn't fair for other reasons?"

"Well, yeah! If life was fair I wouldn't be here. I would be out there," she gestures to the front of the building.

"So, how did you get here?" Janet asks.

"My mom and dad said if I didn't come here I had to go to Iowa with my grandparents."

"Is that the first time they have threatened to send you away?" Janet asks.

"No. They ship me off to my grandparents whenever they think I'm too much to handle."

"What's the message you take away from that?"

"You mean, what do I think about that?"

"Yeah. What does that tell you about how they see you?"

"They think I'm a pain in the ass, and probably regret having me. I was adopted you know."

"How long have you known you are adopted?"

"I don't know. I always knew. They told me this meant I was special, but I think it means, 'It's not our fault – she's not our gene pool!" she says emphatically.

"Do they have any idea you feel this way?" Janet wonders.

"They have no idea how I feel about anything," Cathy says. "They just want me to get my shit together so they can go on with their lives. Honestly, it was always about them anyway. I think they thought having a kid would make them a family, but there's not a lot of room for a kid. They're all about each other."

Janet is struck by her perceptiveness. "You are really a good observer. You probably don't miss much!" Janet smiles

Cathy smiles back. "Not much," she agrees.

"I still don't see how not writing the paragraph fits in," Janet says.

"I don't think you really give a shit what I think either. Why should I bother? I'll be here 30 days and then I'll bounce. I am just one more file for you to fill out." Cathy explains.

Janet is struck by how articulately the young woman describes what she has felt inside herself her whole life. She finds herself admiring Cathy.

"You know what, Cathy. I totally relate to that feeling. I've even said stuff like that in my own head. You know what MY therapist says to me?"

"You have a therapist too?"

Janet nods. "She says, "Would you know how to handle it if they did care? Maybe you're afraid to find out."

Cathy stares at her. "Are you?"

"I'm not totally sure. Are you?"

"I'm not totally sure," Cathy smiles.

"Well, since neither one of us is totally sure, why don't you do an experiment and write your paragraph and see what happens. You have nothing to lose," Janet challenges her.

Cathy gets up, "I'll think about it," she says as she heads back to group.

"What a trip," Janet thinks as she watches Cathy leave. *"Sarah's right, she's a cool kid."* This reminds her that Sarah is on duty tonight with Eddie. *"I think I'll grab Sarah and see if we can arrange time with Cathy over the weekend."*

She charts her meeting with Cathy and is finishing up when Ricardo and Jesse come in.

"Did J.P deign to join the DBT group?" Janet asked Ricardo.

"He did. Late, so he could make an entrance. But he did."

"Okay, well it's Community group time. Let's see what's going on," Janet said as Ricardo, Jesse, and Keisha head over to the group room.

Community Group

The clients were mostly seated as the counselors entered the room, including J.P. Janet opened up the group with the usual one feeling word check-in, and J.P. threw out, "pissed."

"So this is the time when we check in with concerns and appreciations about the household. Anybody have a concern?" she asks.

Donna says, "It feels really tense in here today. It makes me a little anxious."

"Do you know what the anxiety is about?" Janet prompts her.

"It just feels like something's going to jump off, like when I was growing up with my alcoholic mother."

Janet nodded. "I know the feeling. Anybody else feel what Donna's describing?"

Alan, Angie, and Lonnie nod.

"So what's your guess about where the tension's coming from?"

"I think it's J.P.," Tony says. Janet thinks to herself that he probably feels braver because he is a little older so he can see what a poser the guy is. Some of the younger people may have bought into some of J.P.'s prison stories.

J.P. gives him the stink eye. "Pay attention to your own business, old man," he mutters.

"Why do you think Tony may have singled you out, J.P.?" Ricardo asks.

"I don't know what the loser's problem is. I do know he's gonna have a problem if he doesn't shut the f**k up," he threatens.

Janet can feel Jesse tense up next to her and she makes a tiny gesture to him to 'wait.'

Threatening another resident is a deal breaker in most treatment centers. It jeopardizes the safety of the house and makes the vulnerability required to heal impossible. So, at this point J.P. isn't giving the staff a lot of choice in their response. Meanwhile the house becomes very quiet. Ricardo looks at Janet.

"Oh, of course you're looking at me. Honestly, why do I always have to have bigger balls than everyone else in the room?" Janet sighs to

herself.

"Okay, well that's a deal breaker, J.P. At this point, I'm going to have you step into the office with Ricardo who'll call the Clinical Director. We'll have a meeting, and make a decision about where to go with your treatment from here."

J.P. doesn't move.

"You either need to do it now, or I call 911 and we have the cops handle it. It's your choice," she says as she pulls out her cell phone.

J.P. shoots another hater look at Tony, and follows Ricardo into the office. He plants himself in Janet's chair as Ricardo calls the Clinical Director.

J.P. and Ricardo

Ricardo calls the Clinical Director. "Good morning. We have a situation here that requires your expertise, sir. We've had a client threaten another client, who's sitting with me now in the office. I'll hang with him here until you arrive," Ricardo says.

J.P. is looking nonchalant.

"Jesus, what is Janet doing?" the Clinical Director snaps into the phone.

"She's finishing Community group with Keisha and Jesse. Then she'll join us."

"Okay," the Clinical Director sighs as he thinks to himself, *"this guy is such a pussy."*

"I'll come right over."

Ricardo wouldn't be surprised to hear that the Clinical Director thinks of him as a pussy. He knows it's often true. Even though he knows having a raging father taught him to hold his peace, he still hasn't learned that the choices aren't either raging or silence. That's why he had a desire to "bitch slap" a client earlier today. His adrenal system shoots up quickly in the face of conflict and he sometimes actually dissociates, as do many trauma victims. He leaves his body which allows him to physically calm down but not respond in the moment.

Meanwhile, Janet is debriefing with the clients.

"Okay, how are you guys doing?"

"I'm a little worried about Tony," says Lonnie. "That guy's been to prison," she says.

Tony smiles at her. "That guy is a punk and was probably someone's girlfriend when he was in there."

"Hey, wait a minute. . ." Donna says.

"I'm sorry Donna. I didn't mean to offend you. I was just trying to make a point."

"I think your point is that you don't feel particularly threatened?" Janet clarifies.

"Exactly. He's no big deal, except in his own mind."

"Well, I just want peace. Since that guy came in it's been hard," says Alan. "If he stays, can he be less stressful for everyone?"

"Yeah, like wash his own dish?" Cathy asks.

Janet doesn't want this to dissolve into J.P. bashing, and she is getting some great threads to follow in Process group later.

"I am going to ask you to trust us to handle this in a way that is best for everyone involved. You will be safe here, that's a promise," Janet reassured them.

After checking in a little further, the group was pretty subdued as it broke up, and she sees the Clinical Director pull up. "*Here we go,*" she thinks to herself.

He breezes on in and greets a few clients. He sees Janet and they enter the office together.

"So, Ricardo, what's happening here?" the Clinical Director asks while eyeing J.P.

The Work Goes On

'We haven't met, I'm the Clinical Director here," he says to J.P. as he shakes his hand. J.P. shakes his hand limply.

"Well, we were in Community group. They were expressing a feeling that something is about to "jump off," and Tony points to J.P. as the problem. J.P took exception to this and threatened to cause Tony a problem if he doesn't "shut the f**k up" which we heard to be threatening," Ricardo explains.

"What were you thinking when you threatened Tony?" the Clinical Director asked J.P.

"I was thinking he should mind his own f**king business and stop being such a snitch," J.P. postured.

Janet thinks to herself, "Uh oh. He's posturing with the Synanon king. I see a hot seat coming," she thinks.

"Pretty strong language. Figured he hasn't done time so he might be intimidated by you?" the Clinical Director says. "I've done time. I'm not intimidated by you at all. In fact, inside you were probably an ass-wipe, if you know what I mean?"

J.P. just stared at him, speechless for once.

The Clinical Director turns to Ricardo, "Is this guy a State guy?"

Ricardo nods.

"Hey, I'm not a state guy. I'm private pay."

"YOU don't have any money, son. Your grandmother is private pay. You are a custodial resident of the Correctional department. The question is where you should do the rest of your time. Who's his parole agent?" the Clinical Director asks.

Ricardo checks J.P's file. "It's Johnson, sir"

The Clinical Director eyeballed J.P. "Johnson's a prick. He'd roll you up just to do it, right?" he asks J.P.

J.P. sits very still, which amuses the hell out of Ricardo watching the Clinical Director's performance.

The Work Goes On

"Give me one single reason I shouldn't pick up the phone and call Johnson right now," he asks J.P.

J.P. just stares at him. "I don't want to go back, sir," he says in an unconscious imitation of Ricardo.

"Who does? Why should you stay is my question?"

"I want a chance to stay out. I want a chance to stop being such a dick," J.P. says.

"Bingo!" says the Clinical Director. "That's what I was waiting for. So you DO recognize that you've been a colossal pain in our ass since you got here, and that was a decision on your part. Therefore you can CHOOSE to stop being a pain in the ass?"

J.P. nods. "I can."

"Okay then. You'll start by apologizing to Tony and the group as a whole for your shitty attitude and we'll start over. I get another call, I don't come over I just call Johnson to come roll you up. Got it?"

J.P. nods. "Okay then, go get a smoke before psychoeducation."

J.P. can't leave fast enough and the Clinical Director breaks out in a huge grin. "Man, that's fun! These young guys are such punks. In the old days we would've made him sit in the hot seat and then make him clean the bathroom with a toothbrush to teach him some humility!"

Janet shudders inside when he says things like this, grateful that he lets her handle the situations her way. Though she has to admit, intimidation might just be what J.P. needs. *"We'll see how long it lasts, though,"* she thinks to herself. She bets less than 24 hours.

Janet turns to Jesse. "I felt you tense up in there. What was going on with you?" Janet asks.

"I wasn't even aware of it at first, until you looked at me. I think it was automatic pilot. I'm used to being here alone on the weekends, so I'm the one that has to intervene. It was weird to sit back and let someone else do it. But it was fun to see what you would do," he responds.

"Would you have done anything differently?" Janet asks with curiosity.

Jesse thinks. "If I have been with a CD Tech I would have taken J.P. to the office and left them with the clients. That's the only difference. Then I would have called The Man," Jesse smiles at the Clinical Director.

"Well, my work here is done. I need to head back. Good work people," the Clinical Director says over his shoulder as he leaves the room.

Psychoeducation

Janet grabs her curriculum for Psychoeducation group and Jesse trails her. J.P. is still here and she'll give him a chance to apologize. Then she'll be able to start facilitating.

The clients are still arranging themselves as they enter the group room, and all eyes are on Janet as she sits down.

"Well, as you know we had a meeting with J.P., and I think we have some things a little clearer. J.P. mentioned that he has something he wants to say, so I guess now is as good a time as any, if you want?" Janet suggests.

J.P. sits up a little straighter and looks at Tony. "Dude, I was out of line trying to back you up like that. It won't happen again," J.P. offers.

Tony smiles at him.

"I also want to say that I know I've been a jerk since I got here. I think I'm pissed off about being here instead of straight release because my P.O. thinks I need help with my drug use. I feel like I was forced to be here, and I hate that feeling," he explains.

"I totally get that," Brian says. "My parents said it was here or the street, so I don't feel a lot of choice."

"My husband said it was here or divorce court," Lonnie adds.

"Most people enter treatment under some kind of coercion. If you think about it, giving up your freedom voluntarily is something that most of us never want to do. We either have to be desperate or forced," Janet acknowledges.

"I thought you have to WANT help for recovery to work," Angie says. "How is this going to work if so many of us feel forced to be here?"

"That's an excellent question!" Janet smiles. "You just gave me the opening to today's lecture which is about the addicted brain, and how it heals."

Janet tapes up a large drawing of the inside of the brain, and points to different parts as she speaks.

"How old were you guys when you first started using alcohol or drugs regularly?" she asks a she looks around the room.

"15" "18" "13" "21" "25" gets shouted out.

"Let me tell you why that's important. This back part of your brain is called your brain stem – we also call it the reptilian brain (she makes a lizard comb on top of her head with her hands and sticks out her tongue, which makes them laugh). This is the part that tells us we need to sleep, eat, have sex, breathe. It helps us survive. All living creatures have this part of the brain.

Some creatures evolved to develop this next part of the brain – the midbrain, or the limbic system. This is the seat of our emotions, fight or flight, our memory, our automatic memories. It is also the place where we have our reward system which is run by something called dopamine. Mammals, like cats and dogs, have this brain along with humans.

The part of our brain that makes us human is this front part, the pre-fontal cortex. It's where we have logic, organization, choose our behaviors and have impulse control. This is the part of our brain that helps us think about our thoughts – this is something only human beings do, as far as we know. This part of our brain doesn't fully mature until we are 25 years old.

When you start using drugs and alcohol regularly, you start operating more and more out of your midbrain – your emotions and automatic memory. The part of your brain that remembers how to ride a bicycle is the same part that remembers how to find alcohol and drugs even in a strange town. It's the part that remembers your dealer's number even when you can't recall your mom's. The longer this goes on your reward system convinces your reptilian brain that using alcohol and drugs is necessary for your survival. More important than eating, sleeping, even sex."

"How does it convince it?" Brian asks

"By something called tolerance and withdrawal. Your body starts to feel more normal when you are using than when you're clean. In fact, if you don't use you can get withdrawal symptoms that can even be life threatening, like with alcohol or anxiety meds like Valium. The craving is intense and overrides everything else, right?"

They nod.

"While this shift is taking place, and you are getting more and more physically dependent, you are using your prefrontal cortex less and less. Your judgment is impaired, your planning is poor, and your awareness of consequences is messed up. This is worse if you started using regularly before 25 which means there are life skills and planning skills you aren't learning when everyone else your age is learning them."

"Is that why I feel 16 years old in a 40 year old body?" Donna asks.

"That's exactly why. The good news is that the brain is really flexible and if you stay clean your development will catch up and you will become your own age!" she smiles at the group.

"What does this have to do with feeling forced in here?" Cathy asks.

"Because you're addicted, you're operating out of emotion and survival, and your prefrontal cortex is off-line; you aren't always CAPABLE of choosing to get clean. Your impulse control and craving to use is waaaay stronger than your decision making. Every once in a while you will hear someone in a meeting talk about a "moment of clarity?"

The group nods.

"Every once in a while your prefrontal cortex breaks through and you 'see' yourself clearly. But you could die while waiting for that to happen. So an external intervention, often by family or the judge may be what stops you long enough to let your prefrontal cortex come back online to make better decisions on your own behalf.

This can take months, so counselors and sponsors often act as your external prefrontal cortex until yours is operating better. WE are the impulse control, the planning and organization, the structure until you are ready to take the training wheels off and do life by yourself. Does that make sense?" she asks them.

"So, my parents put me here because they were afraid I would die since I couldn't think for myself?" Brian asks.

"I don't know if they were aware of the disease itself, but they were absolutely afraid you would drink yourself to death before 'asking' for help. Interventions are about 'raising the bottom,' so you don't have to lose everything or live under a bridge. Some people wind up there, but many of us are "rescued" by family, employers, P.O.'s who are hoping we don't have to live under a bridge or become crippled in a DUI while killing someone else."

Janet turns to Tony. "Tony what comes to mind as you're listening to me right now?"

"Several things. I wish I had known my Dad was sick instead of waiting for him to figure it out. If you're right, he couldn't see it himself. He wasn't really 'choosing' to drink the way I would define it." Tony says sadly. "I took it so personally."

"So did I," says Donna. "So did my girlfriend."

"What about your drinking?" Janet asks Tony.

"I'm still not sure I have 'lost control' the way you are describing it. I still am a project manager at work, so I use my prefrontal cortex."

"Your boss makes the connection between your work performance and alcohol. Now that you have more time sober, maybe it would be helpful for you to give him a call and ask him what he was seeing that you weren't able to see at the time. It might be a painful conversation for you, but it might help you have some clarity," she suggests.

Tony nods. "I'll think about it."

Jesse and Janet return to the office after group.

"You were really quiet in there, Jesse. What was going on?" Janet asks him.

"I was thinking I would never learn to say it as easily as you do. Honestly, I was feeling kind of inadequate."

"Man, the worst thing an intern can do is compare themselves to someone with 20 years of experience. You need to compare yourself to YOU or at least another intern."

Jesse smiles.

"When I was first learning to do this I used a lot more notes, and there's nothing wrong with that. There is a lot of detail, and handouts are great to help prompt you as well as the clients. As an exercise, you might want to create your own lecture notes and handouts to use so that you will feel more confident. If you want, I'll take a look and give you feedback. Then we can have you try it out."

"That's a great idea, Janet. I shouldn't trip. I think I'm a little nervous about my one-on-one with Jeff today. What if he starts to talk about the molest in detail?

"What's your Scope of Practice?"

"Alcohol and drugs."

"Exactly. Let him say what he wants to say, assure him you can help with a referral since it is a longer term issue, and bring it back to 'How does this affect your recovery?' When in doubt bring the topic back to your scope of practice where you have expertise, and refer out to other professionals. That'll keep you from getting in over your head. Does that make sense?"

Jesse nods. "I sometimes feel pressure to have the answers."

Janet laughs. "Bubba, I don't have all the answers for my own life. I sure as shit don't have all the answers for them!"

"That's a good point," Jesse laughs with her.

Ricardo enters the room as they were laughing. "Hey, the clients are making lizard combs at each other in the kitchen - you must have done your brain parts lecture," says Ricardo.

"Indeed she did," says Jesse as he makes a lizard comb over his own head.

Ricardo laughs and does it back.

"My lovely wife packed some leftovers for me today that I was microwaving, which put me in the kitchen. So, I am going to get some Facebook time and eat my meatloaf," Ricardo says with satisfaction.

"Yum," says Janet. "I think it's Chinese for me today, she says as she grabs her purse and heads out.

Process Group

Janet can feel her fatigue as she heads into Process Group, *"Probably all that MSG,"* she thinks.

"Jesse, I'll collect the secret paragraphs from yesterday, and then I'd like you to take over if you think you're ready," she asks.

Jesse grins, "Bring it."

As the group settles, Janet asks everyone to turn in their secrets paragraphs from the day before. She notices that Cathy adds hers to the pile, which makes Janet smile.

"Okay, I'll read these later. Thank you for doing them. Any highlights you'd like to share?" she asks.

"I realized that I keep secrets about more things than drugs and alcohol," Brian said.

"So keeping quiet about addiction would seem pretty normal for you?" Janet asks.

Brian nods. "I almost think it's a habit."

"I got really clear how much I hate to be accountable. I hate for people to know my business," Jeff says. "Sometimes I'm secretive for no reason."

"I think the accountability thing is huge for me," Donna says. "I hate to feel pinned down or obligated."

Janet grins at all of them. "Well done! The accountability and emotional honestly piece takes a while to develop in recovery. It's going to take lot of practice to even NOTICE when you're being secretive. You've made a good start."

Janet smiles at Jesse to have him start.

"Good afternoon everybody. Let's go ahead with our check in, and let us know if you need some group time," he opens.

The energy in the room was still fairly low, which is not unexpected given that everyone's adrenal system jumped up earlier when J.P. threatened Tony. The check-in's were pretty straightforward, and as Jesse watched them it occurred to him that they would be better off doing something physical.

"Guys, the energy is low in here. I'm going to grab my one pound ball and while I'm doing that, I want you to go in the backyard and make a circle." The shuffling and squeaking of chairs announced their compliance and everyone trailed outside and did as Jesse asked. When he came back out they looked at him curiously. Janet was just as curious as they were.

The Work Goes On

"Let me explain what we're going to do. This ball weighs one pound, and it's to be tossed underhand only. Before you toss the ball you have to say a client's name and then toss the ball to that client. Beginning with the letter "A." The client you toss it to must say a word out loud that begins with "A" as well as the name of the person **they** will be tossing the ball to. The client that catches the ball will say a word out loud that begins with "B" as well as the name of the person **they** will be tossing the ball to. Continue these steps until the clients reach the letter "Z".

Pretty simple, Huh? But here's where it gets interesting.

- If one of you happens to go out of order with the alphabet, we start from the beginning with the letter A.

- If someone tosses it overhand or drops the ball we start from the beginning with the letter A.

- In addition, you cannot help other clients remember what letter we are on.

- Lastly, you have to toss the ball across from you and not to a person next to you.

"Are you ready to begin?" he asks. "I'll start by tossing the ball to Donna," he says as it tosses it to her. Donna catches it with a grin.

"Okay, give us a word that starts with A," Jesse prompts her.

"Apple," she says, "Tony" and heaves it to Tony, who catches it. "Ball," he says, "Alan" as he tosses it to Alan.

The game continues with several "start overs" which was sometimes met with irritation and sometimes with laughter.

As the game is winding up, Jesse has the group sit down in the grass and asks them, "How many of you felt irritated when Lonnie forgot what letter we were on and we had to start over?"

Several people sheepishly grin. "What I want you to notice is what you were thinking. Was it something like, 'Jeez, how hard can it be? Just focus!'"

The Work Goes On

Several people laugh.

"Okay, when your family sees you get loaded AGAIN, do you ever wonder if they are thinking the same thing? Jeez, how hard can it be? Just don't drink!"

"I KNOW that's what my mom thinks," Angie says. "She says that to me."

"My husband says the same thing," Lonnie adds.

"When you're first learning something new, like a game or how to be sober, there's a lot to remember. Janet talked to us earlier about how we are out of practice using our frontal lobes so we need help and support to keep on track. You guys did a great job, go ahead and break for the afternoon," Jesse says as he closes. He quietly lets Jeff know that he will be available for their one-on-one in about 15 minutes.

Janet notices that the group is slow to break up, some people stay on the grass and talk. *"They really needed something else,"* Janet recognizes to herself.

As Janet and Jesse head back to the office she is grinning. "Ricardo," she says as they enter the office, "Jesse was amazing out there! He had us outside and moving around. They worked as a team. It was exactly the antidote to this morning's conflict."

Janet turns to Jesse, "That was genius!" she says admiringly. "I would never have thought of that."

Ricardo gives Jesse a fist bump. "Man, it sounds like that schooling is paying off!" Ricardo teases him.

Jesse grins back. "I have to go meet with Jeff now. I feel like I'm ready. I think I needed that exercise as much as the clients did," he laughs and he leaves for the smaller office to wait for Jeff.

Janet looks at Ricardo after Jesse leaves. "You know, that guy's a natural. He's comfortable in his own skin. He's way more confident in who he is than I was when I first started." Janet observes.

The Work Goes On

"Well, Dude is an athlete, Mamacita," Ricardo says. "I think it's his comfort zone. It's good he's finding a way to build from his strength. When I was first starting out I was too paranoid about how I looked. I was worried that I would sound stupid. I think it's an advantage that he was a CD Tech before going to school."

Janet nods. "You make a good point. He was comfortable with the environment so just needed to learn new information and more skills. It was ALL new for Sarah when she started out, so she was slower to develop."

"Does Sarah start with Eddie tonight?" Ricardo wonders.

"You know, I think so. I hope Eddie's okay with it. I suggested that the Clinical Director talk to Eddie about it first."

"Well, then he probably did. I just hope he LISTENED to Eddie's response," Ricardo says.

Janet nods, and is reading the secrets paragraphs when Sarah arrives for her evening shift.

"Sarah, just the person I wanted to see!" says Janet.

"What a great greeting!" Sarah laughs.

"I just had a really cool meeting with Cathy and you are right. She is a fabulous kid. She has abandonment stuff up the whazoo, and I think it would be great if you could spend some time with her this weekend after her parents leave on Saturday. I have a feeling that's going to be tough on her."

Sarah grinned. "I would love to. I sat by her in Art therapy yesterday and she was amazing. So I've already started to connect with her. Anything I need to know?"

"They've had a challenging day – conflict between J.P. and Tony that the Clinical Director had to come down and sort out." Janet says.

"You should have seen him!" Ricardo laughs. "Dude is so old school. He would've had him cleaning the bathroom with a tooth brush!"

The Work Goes On

Sarah shuddered. "Are things calmer then?"

"They seem to be," says Janet. "Jesse just had us outside tossing a ball, and it seemed to lighten the mood."

"Well, let me read the log and get caught up before Eddie gets here. I'm so excited about this opportunity," Sarah smiles.

"I hope to hell Eddie is too," Janet thinks.

Janet has a service position at tonight's 6:00 A.A. meeting, so heads across town. She has volunteered to set up the chairs, and this is a 40-50 person speaker meeting. Janet counts it as her weekly exercise. As she's setting up the last row she sees Ronnie, another treatment center operator, sidle in with a group of guys in tow. *"I hate that nubby pony tail"* she thinks. *"What the hell is the point of that thing?"*

Ronnie is a sketchy operator, who can be ethically challenged due to his attachment to his financial bottom line. As usual, he was bringing the guys to a nightly FREE A.A. meeting instead of paying an evening counselor to deliver the program. *"He charges so much money."* Janet thinks. *"How does he get away with that?"*

"Good evening, Janet, can I help?" Ronnie smarms. He's the kind of guy that likes to "glad hand' you; Janet always feels like he is about to try to sell her a condo or used car.

"Hey Ronnie, I think I've got it," Janet murmurs as she offers him a lackluster fist bump to avoid hugging him.

"So, Janet. When are you going to come see me about working for a REAL operation? I could pay you way more than I suspect you're getting over at the nonprofit."

"Wow, Ronnie, I appreciate the vote of confidence. But I really love my team. I can't imagine there's enough money to ever replace them," she adds.

"I don't know, lady, there's a lot of money to be made. It's time you got your share of the pie," Ronnie suggests. "Nothing about recovery says we need to be poor. Aren't we promised freedom from financial insecurity?" he smiles.

Janet smiles at him. "Ronnie, if I ever think I need a bigger piece of pie, I will call you first."

"Good to know," he says as he hands her his card, "I'll look forward to it!" She feels a chill as his gaze suddenly shifts from her eyes to over her shoulder. He's spotted a likely newcomer and is already scheming how he might rope them into coming to treatment or his SLE.

As Janet watched him walk away toward his "mark," working the room as he goes along, she can't help but laugh at how utterly scandalous the guy is. *"He is what he is,"* she thinks to herself as she spots her sponsor at the door and heads over to give her a hug.

FRIDAY

Janet feels better rested as she arrives for work the next morning. She sacrificed a Law and Order episode for the sake of sleep, and she could feel the wisdom in that decision as she heads up the driveway.

Janet waves at Jorge as she opens the office door and grabs the log book to read while eating her yogurt. She was feeling particularly self-satisfied today having decided on yogurt instead of a donut. *"Jeez, I need more of a life if this is my big victory for the week,"* she giggles to herself.

There were surprisingly few comments from Eddie, and Sarah reported a positive communication group that evening. J.P. remained cooperative, at least on the surface. The only tension had been the usual squabbling over the remote. If Janet had her way there would be no television in the center at all. It's a pet peeve of hers that clients will try to watch violence, usually drug crime related shows and movies to jack up their dopamine systems. She HAD put a stop to watching "Breaking Bad," and insisted that they watch something else. She was continually outnumbered over this, though she had enjoyed a smirk when the clients found a way to engage pay-per-view and ran up the bill watching special pay-per-view fights! The Clinical Director had been predictably furious, and disabled the cable box to prevent it from happening again.

As she was mulling this over Ricardo arrived, running late and full of good humor. "Good morning, my friend! Happy Friday"

"Good morning to you. And why is today so particularly happy for you?" Janet asks.

"Because I'm going to be a father!" he grins.

"Wow! Congratulations," Janet offers as she gave him a hug. "How far along is Josie?"

"She thinks about two months. We did the home pregnancy test last night, and she has a doctor's appointment this afternoon. He'll be able tell us then. I am hoping to sneak out and join her there."

"I don't see why not? I usually do process group, so we should be able to make it work," Janet says.

"What's all the excitement about?" asks Jorge as he enters the room and locks up the client's medications.

"I'm going to be a father!" Ricardo announces.

Jorge gives Ricardo a recovery hug, "Congratulation, bro. Your life is about to change."

Janet notices it is time for Assignment group, so heads across the hall to the group room.

As she's crossing the hall she can feel her heart sink like a stone, remembering how she found out about David's new baby. Someone casually mentioned how much it looked like David, was even named for David, and it took everything in her to stay seated and not run screaming from the room. Instead she smiled politely, and then bought a pumpkin pie on the way home. It was the first time she had felt like drinking in many years, so chose the pie as the lesser of the evils. It took her days to stop hurting, and she didn't even want a child! Well, truthfully, maybe she would have had one with him.

Assignment Group

Assignment group is an opportunity for clients to share assignments such as relapse prevention plans or powerlessness and unmanageability. Sometimes they share their autobiographies.

Tony is scheduled to share his Relapse Prevention plan since he is scheduled to graduate from the program on Saturday. Janet asks him to go first.

Tony begins by saying, "I'm still not sure I'm an alcoholic, but after talking to my boss, I can see where I haven't been as sharp as I used to be, and I really was tired a lot of the time. I really wasn't on my game, and drinking to help the stress probably wasn't the best idea. So here's what I came up with."

The Work Goes On

Identifying slippery places and situations which can hurt my recovery

Situations and places that are dangerous for my recovery:

1. __Sports bar for lunch_____
2. __Working too much_____
3. __Getting pissed off at my boss _
4. __Holding resentments against my co-workers___
5. __Not getting enough sleep_____

How will I cope with each of the above situations:

1. __Pick up lunch at a non-drinking place_____
2. __Try to plan things to do after work, like hit some balls__
3. __Keep things in perspective and stay on top of my ego_
4. __Check my expectations of other people_____
5. __Keep a regular bedtime___

Check off any of these warning signs that might apply to you.

- __ Bored most of the time
- X Avoiding problems
- X Problems sleeping
- __ Missing meetings and aftercare
- X Blaming other people
- __ Dreaming of the "good old days"
- X Visiting taverns and bars
- __ Being uncommunicative
- __ Not taking action
- __ Keeping a stash just in case
- X Thinking, I can handle it on my own
- __ Dwelling on mistakes
- X holding onto resentments

The Work Goes On

- [X] Keeping secrets
- [ ] Lying about activities
- [X] Hanging out with drinking friends
- [ ] Thinking you are cured
- [ ] Quitting therapy
- [ ] Missing appointments
- [ ] Stopping medications
- [ ] Getting too hungry
- [X] Excess Anger
- [ ] Staying too lonely
- [ ] Being too tired
- [ ] Quit reading recovery literature
- [X] Worrying too much about the future

What I will do if I want to drink or use?

Call my sister

Go to aftercare

Get a personal counselor

Go for a run w/my dog

Read or go to a movie

Go to an AA meeting

_____

_____

Make a list of things to do that are enjoyable and healthy.

Go to a ball game

_____

_____

Janet opens the group for feedback.

"I was relieved to hear something about getting support," Donna says. "I noticed you would go to AA as a last resort, but at least you put it down!" she laughs.

"I think it was really consistent with how you feel about addiction. It's cool how honest you are being about not knowing. You're not blowing smoke up anyone's skirt," says Alan.

"I hear that you have a lot of free time if you don't drink after work, so it's good that you're thinking ahead about how to fill the time," says Jeff. "I took a note about some of the things you mentioned because they would work for me too."

"I think you've done a really authentic job, and I have a lot of respect for your consistency, Tony," Janet says." I am glad you've agreed to attend weekly aftercare, because I would like us to be part of your support system, and you're right that you CAN call during the week if you get stuck. As you know, we're here 24 hours a day!" she says laughing.

"I also want to give you props for calling your boss. That couldn't have been easy. But it sounds like you took his feedback to heart, and plan to do things differently" Janet adds.

"However, I have a concern that you still feel like you're fully in control of your drinking, which is a set up for you to get yourself back in trouble. How will you know you're no longer in control of your drinking? What sign will you have?" Janet asks.

Tony thinks a minute. "If I decide I am not going to drink, and then I do. If I decide I am not going to have lunch at the sports bar but then I do."

"So if you start breaking commitments you make to yourself?" Janet clarifies.

"Exactly. I stop being able to predict when I will drink. I think you said the lack of predictability is one of the hallmarks of alcoholism. We are never sure how much we will drink or when, right?"

"I did say that. I love it when you guys are listening!" she grins.

Janet listens to a few more assignments and then stops by the office before Community Group. Ricardo is on Facebook still posting about his baby and answering congratulations posts from other people. Normally this would annoy her, but today she finds herself smiling at him.

"Are your 500 Facebook friends excited for you?" she asks him.

"Si, they are. They're saying that they hope I have a son because I would never let my daughter date!" he says laughing.

"That reminds me of a T-shirt I saw the other day. It said, D.A.D.D. – Dad's Against Daughter's Dating," Janet teases him.

Ricardo grins, "I should order one now!"

"Well I need to pull you away from your friends so we can meet Jorge for Community Group. I can hear them shuffling the chairs around even now."

"Okay," he says as he logs off. "I'll have more to report later anyway."

Community Group

Ricardo, Janet and Jorge arrive for Community group, and Janet notices that J.P. seems to be missing. She decides to give it a couple minutes then slip away to check on him if he doesn't show up. As the clients are going around the group checking in, J.P. lands in his seat to be the last person to check-in.

"I'm good," he says.

"I notice you were running late, J.P." Ricardo says. "What's up?"

J.P. looks irritated. "I had to take a shit, okay? Can't we have any privacy? I feel like I'm back in lock up," he mutters.

"There he is," Janet thinks.

Ricardo is surprised by the intensity of his defensiveness, as are the other clients.

The Work Goes On

"Dude, that was a lot of heat for a simple question."

J.P. just shrugs and stretches his legs out in front of him.

Ricardo looks at the rest of the group. "The group's open for concerns and appreciations. Does anyone have anything?" he prompts.

"I have something," Alicia says. "I'm feeling cooped up, and am wondering if we can spend some time at a park this weekend if the weather's okay. It would be nice see something besides each other – no offense guys."

Everyone laughs. "None taken," says Alan. "I feel the same way."

"Let me talk to Jesse about the weekend schedule and see what we can do. I think we can figure something out," Janet says.

"Oh, we need more paper towels for the kitchen, says Donna. "And someone has had a Tupperware bowl in there since last Saturday and I think whatever was in it is pretty gross by now."

"Well, cleaning the fridge is part of double scrub and everything that's left over gets tossed anyway," Jorge reminds them. "So if someone is saving a science project in there, be warned!" he laughs.

The group continues in a house keeping vein and there are a couple of appreciations before closure.

Janet and Ricardo head into the office so Ricardo can get his curriculum binder. Janet has asked Lonnie to meet with her for a one-on-one in a few minutes.

"So, I see J.P. has rejoined us," Janet smiles. "Actually, I lost a bet with myself because I thought he'd be back in 24 hours after we met with the Clinical Director and he lasted 2 days" she adds.

"Yeah, the hostility was weird. I'm thinking dude is plotting and scheming, what do you think?"

"I think your instincts are right on. He's up to something.

Fortunately he can't manage his anxiety, so he'll give himself up sooner or later. I'm not thrilled to see the posturing return. I'm really glad it's Friday and I'm going to get a break from it."

Ricardo nods. "Yeah, it can be an energy drag. Well, here I go," he says as he crosses the hall to psychoeducation group. Janet hears a knock on the door and Lonnie enters.

Lonnie

"Hi Lonnie. I wanted to follow up on our conversation in women's group about your relationship with your husband, and using pills to give yourself permission to speak your mind. Remember that?" Janet opens.

"That seems so long ago, and it's only been 4 days," Lonnie laughs. "But yeah, I remember that. Honestly the closer it gets to Saturday Family group the more nervous I get."

"You mentioned feeling guilty about the money your arrest has cost you and his extra work with childcare?"

"You know, the kids are 13 and 15, so they aren't toddlers. But he acts like he has to supervise them as though they were! At their age they have afterschool activities and would rather be with their friends. I have to round them up at night to settle them down to do homework because they would rather be texting or on the computer. That's the level of supervision we're talking about!" she states with emphasis.

"I get it. That's probably why your using could increase. You had more free time other than shuttling them around. I get the feeling that your husband didn't know the full extent of your using until you called him from the police station. Is that right?"

"I'm sure that's right. We lived pretty parallel lives. Most of our conversation has become logistical. He had no idea how much time I was spending seeing doctors because our insurance was covering everything and the co-pays were low."

"How did he feel about your 'secret'? Sometimes our family is angrier about the secrets and lies than they are about the using itself," Janet asks.

"The only feeling he expresses to me is anger, and maybe judgment. I honestly don't know how he felt about finding out. He focused on the attorney expenses

"Would you feel safe enough to ask him?"

"I don't know. I already have so much guilt, I don't know if I can take any-more heaped on."

"What if you knew that letting him get it out was a gift to him so he could heal?"

"I guess I could do it then, but I would want support."

"That's what our family counselor Kym is for. You can meet with her as a couple. Is your husband going to bring your daughters?' Janet asks.

"I don't know. Aren't they too young? I don't know if I want them to learn about me," she says. "Maybe they won't respect me anymore," she says as she starts to tear up.

"Why do they think you're here?" Janet asks.

"I'm not sure what my husband told them. He did say last night that they wanted to see me."

"I'm sure they do. They're old enough for your husband to tell them you're getting help to stop taking so many pills. I know they know you take pills."

Lonnie smiles, "They call them my 'nerve pills'."

"Well, I encourage your husband to bring the girls. You can have lunch and they can watch TV while you meet with Kym as a couple. They need to heal also. They've noticed that you weren't always there, and it will comfort them to see that you're changing this."

"You think they really noticed?" Lonnie asks with wide eyes.

"Well, Lonnie, I'd be surprised if they didn't. Kids notice

everything about their parents, especially their availability. You can ask them yourself tomorrow." Janet suggests.

"This is so hard. I really wish I could just treat this like a normal illness. Take a pill or have a surgery and it would be over."

"Yeah, this one is going to take a life change."

"What a pain in the ass," Lonnie sighs.

Janet just nods.

Janet is finishing her charting when Ricardo barrels into the office. He looks aggravated.

"Wow, someone licked the red off your candy, as my mother used to say. What's happened?"

Ricardo shoves his curriculum into the shelf and sits heavily in his chair.

"You member when Cathy told you to F-off on Monday?"

"Oh yeah. A great start to my day."

"So I am talking to the group about expectations, reasonable and unreasonable expectations, and how they are premeditated resentments."

Janet nods.

"Suddenly, miss eyeliner points out that she has an 'expectation' that her counselor should be able to spell, and starts ragging on me about my typos! This gets J.P. going, who takes the opportunity to chime in that he 'expects' to take a shit without a third degree. It was all I could do not to smack both of them in the middle of group!" he says heatedly.

Janet shook her head in sympathy. Clients will frequently take pot shots at staff to redirect the conversation when they are uncomfortable or to attempt to establish control in an arena where they are not feeling control. People in early recovery are remarkably self-centered and lack empathy about their impact on the staff or others in treatment. This is one of the more unpleasant addict/alcoholic traits, and pushes people away from them over time. People get tired of the addict's self-centeredness.

"I know, it really gets old," Janet says with sympathy. "It's even harder when you were having such a happy day," Janet adds.

"I told you I was going to have to do a Fourth step about that guy, didn't I?" Ricardo asks more calmly.

Janet smiles, "Indeed you did. You saw that train coming."

Ricardo sighs. "This is why this is a J.O.B. and not a hobby right?"

"Yeah, it's stuff like this that makes us demand a paycheck and not just do it for the 'love of service'," Janet agrees.

"You know what? I think you should meet your wife for lunch and get your vibe back. Then take her to her appointment. We will see you back here after that. What do you think?" Janet asks.

"What a great idea! You're the bomb. I'll call her and let her know I'm on the way to pick her up. I'll be back in a couple of hours." Ricardo says with a smile. He leaves with a lighter step.

Janet smiles to herself as she turns back to her computer and decides to check the news to remind herself of the world out there beyond her little corner.

Process Group

Janet and Jesse start off the Process Group with the usual check-in, and Janet finds herself watching J.P. out of the corner of her eye. She decides to open the discussion by bringing up an addict's tendency to distract and defocus when they are uncomfortable or do not want to be held accountable.

"I know Family day is tomorrow, and sometimes conversations can be a little sticky during visitation. Sometimes your family will want to talk about things you've said or done that are bothering them, and I encourage you to watch out for ways you attempt to distract or defocus them. Can you think of times you did this when you were using?" Janet asks.

"I know I do it with my Mom, "Angie says. "She has a tone of voice she uses that tells me she's about to lecture me or ask me something I don't want to talk about and I'll start fussing with my son, or remembering I need to do something else to get out of it."

"I'll accuse my wife of nagging or being controlling, and she starts to defend herself and drops the topic," Jeff admits.

"I've started fights about something else to get my girlfriend to stop asking me about my drinking and using," Donna adds.

"Does anyone escalate – make situations way worse or create crisis to distract them?" Janet asks.

"My girlfriend does that," Brian says. "I can tell when Brittany doesn't want to talk about something because she'll start to ask me if I love her or accuse me of looking at other women. Pretty soon we're fighting about that! I never thought of it before as a tactic," Brian says.

"Oh, God, I hate when women do that!" Alan laughs.

"We wouldn't do it if you would listen to us in the first place, "Lonnie quips.

"Wait a minute, we'll tackle gender stuff later. I am talking about an addict/alcoholic's attempts to avoid accountability – the same reason we keep secrets and tell half-truths," Janet clarifies.

"Do you think any of you has done that with us while you've been in treatment? Asked a question in group to change the subject, or blame us for something so we wouldn't stick to the subject and get defensive?" Janet asks

"Oh, I know what this is about," says Cathy, "Ricardo must have been whining about us busting his balls in group earlier," Cathy laughs.

"Perhaps. If it is about that, can you remember what Ricardo may have been talking about that might have made you feel uncomfortable – like pushing him away?" Janet asks.

Cathy pouts a minute then says, "Now you're busting my balls."

"Actually, I'm just being curious. Do you remember the topic?" she persists.

"We were talking about expectations and resentment," offers Angie

"Okay. So, Cathy, what about expectations or resentment may have made you a little uncomfortable?" Janet asks.

"Nothing, I was just playing," Cathy mutters.

"I give you more credit than that. I think you're pretty smart and used to influencing situations with what you say and do. Whose resentment or expectations were you thinking about when you got snarky with Ricardo?"

"Okay, then. He reminded me of my mom and dad when they lecture me about their disappointment because I didn't meet their 'expectations.' It pisses me off when they do that. I always feel like saying to them, "Fine, take me back to the orphanage~"

"Have you ever said that?" Janet asks.

"Maybe. Probably. They're so self-righteous. They make me sick!"

"Do they have any idea how much you are always waiting for them to send you back?" Jesse asks

Cathy looks at him. "I don't think they even think about what I'm thinking."

"I get that. My parents had such a shitty divorce and instant remarriages that I spent all my time with my grandma. They barely even knew I existed, other than someone they had to 'make arrangements' for, like finding a good kennel for the family dog!" J.P. sputtered.

"Wow, man. That must have been harsh," Jesse empathized.

"Yeah, it was a long time ago. I don't even know why I said anything."

"Maybe you said something because it is the way you feel about people in general," Janet posed.

"You mean that they think they don't want me?"

"Yeah, that you're disposable. Anyone else ever feel disposable?" Janet asks the group.

"I certainly feel like my husband was willing to throw me out of the family if I didn't come here," Lonnie says.

"My parents said it was here or the streets," says Brian.

"So part of healing and staying clean and sober is learning to trust that relationships can be stable, that people can stick with you for the long haul. It's a matter of trusting the attachments you form with other people. Otherwise you only trust your attachment to alcohol and drugs. Substances are reliable and predictable, but not people. That's the theme," Janet observes.

"That's what you said to me earlier this week. That I trusted alcohol more than I trusted my girlfriend," Donna says.

"Yeah, that's where I was going," Janet agreed. "What do you guys think about that?" she asks.

"I think that's a good point. It's probably one of the reasons I always want to have alcohol around the house somewhere. I feel better just knowing it's there," Alan says.

"Great observation, Alan. Anyone else?"

This was a tough discussion for Janet to facilitate because it touches a core issue. Feeling disposed of and replaced by the bimbo is a key to her despair. She felt profoundly devalued and undesirable when her world fell apart, and only now is she understanding the childhood set up for her despair when being dumped confirmed what she always knew – 'I'm not worth choosing.' Her mom chose alcohol, her dad chose work, and the first time she chose herself was her decision to get and stay sober after her near-death accident. Continuing to choose herself is an ongoing battle.

The Work Goes On

When Jesse and Janet got back to the office after Process group, Ricardo had returned and was on the phone. As they came in, he turned in his chair beaming.

"Look!" he says as he holds out a sonogram. "There's the baby!"

"What gender is the child?" Janet asks.

"I don't know, we asked the doctor not to tell us. We want to be surprised. But I'm not sure I can wait 7 months, so I may cave and find out. We'll see!" he grins.

"I see a Facebook posting coming," teases Jesse.

"Already happening, dude. Why do you think I am glued to the computer?"

Janet opens her screen to her charting file. "Well, some of us are glued to the charting file. Then again some of us have lives," she smiles.

"Why am I always saying that?" Janet asks herself. *"I am always acting like I have no life, when I clearly do. I have my work, my recovery, my friends, my hobbies. It's like I don't have a life because I don't have a relationship with David anymore. HE has a life because he has a new family. Single people don't have lives. That's bullshit, I need to stop saying that!"* she chides herself.

Janet checks her voicemail and picks up a message from Eddie. "Hi Janet. I'm not going to make it in tonight. I'm sure Sarah will be just fine. Thanks."

Janet could feel her stomach knot as she listened again to the message, *"I was afraid of this,"* she thinks.

As she's hanging up the phone Sarah arrives for the evening session.

"Hey there," Janet greets Sarah. "Eddie's not going to make it in tonight. You're on your own in class."

Sarah looks worried. "I'm going to be here by myself? Normally there's two of us on duty."

Janet thinks a moment. "Let me check with Keisha and see if she can stay. I don't want you alone for the evening until Carl gets here," Janet says as she heads out to the main lounge area.

"Keisha, Eddie called in and Sarah needs a second person on shift. I know you have been here all day. Are you up for some overtime?"

Keisha looked torn. "I guess... but I told my boyfriend we would try the new sushi place. I haven't given him much time lately, so he's been feeling frustrated with me."

Janet thought to herself, *"It's Friday, and I can sleep in tomorrow before my women's meeting at 10:00. I can manage this."*

"It's okay, Keisha. I have some paperwork to get to anyway, and I still need to call Kym with the download for tomorrow. Go ahead and enjoy your evening," Janet smiles.

Keisha grinned gratefully, and headed into the office to log out and collect her purse.

Janet follows Keisha into the office and says to Sarah, "Okay, doll. It's you and me. I have some work to do anyway, so I'll handle pill call and prep Kym for tomorrow," and walks over to the medication cabinet.

Treatment center staff prepare the medications for the clients to dispense to themselves since staff are not medical personnel. Sometimes they simply hand the client the pill bottle and the client takes the pills as prescribed, and sometimes they prepare the pills in cups and the clients take the cup from the staff.

Medications are logged every time they are admitted initially, and every time the client takes a pill. It is a running count, and the staff member preparing the pills counts the remaining pills in the bottle every time. This is how Eddie was discovered over a year ago. Carl discovered the pill count was not matching the log.

Janet was busy counting pills as Sarah was preparing for the evening group. She is interrupted by a call from Kym to check in.

"Hey, girlfriend, I was waiting for you to rescue me from class. You let me stay the whole time," Kym opens laughing.

"Oh, man, I should not have let that happen – my bad!" Janet laughs.

Kym the Family counselor is completing her marriage, family and child counseling degree at a local graduate school. She is the ex-wife of an alcoholic/Bipolar husband who is maintaining his sobriety, but not doing as well managing his Bipolar disorder. She shares custody of their Asperger's son with him, and she is still insisting on supervision by his parents during the visits, much to her ex's irritation. However, it is the only way she feels safe enough to concentrate on her studies at school or on duty on Saturdays for Family day.

"Indeed it is," Kym says. "What do I have to look forward to tomorrow?"

Janet opens the log to make sure she remembers the highlights. "We had a new admit last Sunday, Brian –"

"The one with the meth girlfriend?"

"That's the one. He is completely absorbed with this girl, fully merged, and is in withdrawal without her. He's easily as addicted to her as he is to alcohol or cocaine. He is expecting her to come with his parents since she can't drive after her DUI. This should be challenging because they can't stand her. In fact, he thinks they admitted him to get him away from her."

"Did he tell her she needs to be clean and we can test?"

"I had him text her with the info. So, we'll see. I've encouraged Lonnie to have her husband bring her daughters, 13 and 15 to family group. She isn't sure what he's told them, but they're aware she was taking what they call "nerve pills" and they need to talk to her. She's pretty nervous, but it needs to happen. She also needs to meet with you and her husband to talk with him about how he's doing. Apparently guilt is his favorite approach, so she needs to see there's more there."

"Yeah, I noticed he was pretty judgmental last week. I can see where she would be coming from with that," Kym says.

"I'm hoping you can find some time with the young girl, Cathy, and her parents. She's adopted and has felt tenuous about the attachment her whole life. She really needs help connecting with them."

"Is that the family that's thinking about the wilderness program? Her parents weren't there last week, so I haven't met them. Yes, I will find time. Anything else?"

"We have a new state guy, J.P. who's been a shit disturber all week. His grandmother is his enabler and chief, and will be there. He wants her to bring all manner of exercise equipment and supplements which we have not okayed. It's possible you may have to direct grandma to leave the crap in the car, and he may have a tantrum."

"Oh, great!"

Janet laughs, "You will not be bored."

"No ma'am I won't! That's for the update. I'll let you know what happens."

"More is always revealed, my friend," Janet giggles as she hangs up. Janet turns to Sarah and says,

"I want to be her when I grow up. I love that woman!"

Sarah nods in agreement, and Janet returns to counting pills.

SATURDAY

Kym arrives with tension in her stomach dreading potential struggles with the new client and his grandmother. This part, the enforcement part, is the hardest for her and she's comforted when she sees Jesse's Harley in the driveway.

Kym has experienced tremendous conflict with her ex-husband, particularly when he was manic and drunk, and she's aware that she can still be hyper-reactive in the face of escalation. In fact, she flinches. While she's not afraid of clients physically, her body goes into automatic fight or flight when voices are raised too high, an artifact of her previous trauma.

"Hey, Jesse. I'm really happy to see you!" Kym greets Jesse. "What's the mood of the house?"

"So far so good. They're setting up the chairs for the family portion of the morning. Some of the clients seem a little tense, but they're holding their own."

"Janet gave me quite a to-do list last night. I'm somewhat concerned about the new guy, the guy with the exercise stuff," she comments as she's reading the log.

Jesse laughs, "Mr. entitled? Don't worry, I can take him AND his grandmother" he grins.

"That's okay – I'll take grandma if it comes down to it, I've been taking kickboxing," she giggles.

There's a knock at the door, and Cathy walks in, "I need to call my mom and remind her to bring my jeans." The clients don't have access to the phone until after family visiting.

"Okay, but they're probably on their way here already," Kym suggests, and hands her the phone.

Cathy dials, "Hey. Don't forget to bring my jeans, okay? What do you mean you're already almost here – I need them! Yeah,

I think you should go back – FINE!" she says as she slams the phone in the cradle.

"Bitch," she mutters and storms out.

"Wow. That was an intense exchange," Kym says.

"Well, my guess is she's on your list to see, right?' Jesse asks.

Kym nods. "Hopefully she'll allow it. We'll see."

They hear the front door opening, and Jesse heads out to make sure the visitors are signing in and checking their bags. Families are not always savvy about what might be appropriate for treatment. Jesse has run across bags of coffee, porn, alcohol based mouthwash, a rice cooker! So, he never trusts common sense to prevail.

He's always interested to watch the family members greet each other. They can be wary, careful of what to say, and always seem awkward. Many addicts and alcoholics lack social skills in the best of circumstances, so conversations quickly devolve into clients telling stories about other people in treatment instead of talking about themselves. The family members share gossip about other people as well, so the disconnect can be obvious to the observer. He can feel how badly they want this to work for the addict in their lives, and his heart goes out to them because the relapse rate in the disease is so high.

Jesse remembers greeting his parents in treatment. The awkward hugs, telling them he's fine, reassuring them that it will all be okay. He remembers them making small talk, and filling the time with TV watching to avoid the silence. He was so resentful then, feeling 'picked on' by their intervention. He felt their concern for him was intrusive, and he felt it embarrassing. He remembers feeling shame when he looked at his hard working parents, knowing that they had scraped together the money to make this opportunity for him. He remembers feeling like a complete shit head, yet grateful they still loved him.

Kym looks out the window and sees Lonnie's husband, Jim and her two daughters arriving. Pulling up behind them are Cathy's parents. A beautiful, older model jaguar pulls up across the street and a stately, elderly woman emerges, pulling a large bag out her trunk and moves up the driveway.

"That must be her," Kym thinks.

She can hear the clients coming out to greet their family members, and sees a sedan pull up with a couple and a young, "goth-looking" girl. *"Wonder if that's the meth girlfriend"*, she thinks as she looks down at the log, *"Brittany. I can't call her meth girlfriend,"* she giggles to herself.

Kym sees Jesse greet Angie's mother, who's bearing a large plate of home-made enchiladas, which makes Kym grin. "I love this part of Saturday."

J.P. comes out to greet his grandmother. "Grandma – cool – you remembered the stuff I wanted!" he says as he hugs her briefly.

Jesse steps up, "Excuse me, ma'am? I need to check your bag," he says to her while reaching for the sack.

J.P. steps in between them, "Dude, back up off my Grandma!" he says aggressively.

Jesse addresses J.P.'s grandmother, "Ma'am, the staff made decisions earlier this week about bringing in extra supplements and exercise equipment, and J.P. was told to inform you that you were not supposed to bring them. So, if you did I am going to have to ask you to put them back in your car."

J.P's grandmother nods and hands over the bag. J.P. starts to challenge Jesse, and his grandmother puts her hand on his arm. "It must've slipped your mind, son. I'm sure you just forgot to call me with so much going on," she says to J.P.

J.P. shakes her hand off his arm and storms back to his room. His grandmother just sighs and settles in a chair for Family group.

Tony's sister, Tina, has arrives to support him at his coin ceremony since he's finishing the residential portion of his program today.

Most of the family has arrived and Kym has decided to introduce a discussion about enabling versus support.

The Work Goes On

"Good morning everyone," she opens smiling. "Thank you for taking time out of your lives to be here and support the people you love. Addiction is a family illness, and one of most confusing issues you face is trying to tell the difference between Enabling and Helping. Let me give you a couple of quick definitions," and she turns to write on the white board:

- **Helping** is doing something for someone else that they are not capable of doing for themselves.

- **Enabling** is doing things for someone else that they can and should be doing for themselves.

"Knowing the difference is hard work. For example it's easy to throw money at an issue and think, *"Well, I've done my part. What they do with it isn't my problem."* Maybe not, but continually giving without following up on where you money is going is your problem. Yes, doing so is a hassle, but if you're continually buying groceries for a kid who doesn't know how to manage his money you aren't helping. Can any of you relate to this?"

Several family members raise their hands.

"I get confused because Angie tells me she's a grown woman and I shouldn't be in her business," Angie's mother, Carmen, says.

"Yeah, but they're quick to make it your business when they NEED money, aren't they?" Cathy's father laughs.

"I keep thinking if I give J.P a good attorney or a good treatment program he can get a fresh start and get his life together," says J.P.'s grandmother, Lucille.

"I really do understand what you're saying. We struggle with how to parent our adult children or treat our spouses like adult partners when they aren't acting like adults." Kym acknowledges. So let's take a look at a few reasons why we get in these situations," she continues and turns to the board and writes:

We think suffering is always bad.

"As parents we're hard wired to protect our children, it's our JOB. As spouses we have taken vows to be there, for better or worse. It's incredibly hard to see someone we love be uncomfortable or make really bad decisions. The powerlessness can be almost physically painful. Can any of you relate?" she asks.

Lonnie's husband, Jim, says, "I don't understand it. Why is she willing to go to jail, leave the girls and me, and check out on us all the time? She doesn't take care of herself, and nothing I can say or do has made any difference," he says with frustration.

"It's like talking to a brick wall," Cathy's mother Karen says. "I watch her throw away opportunity after opportunity, almost like she WANTS to wind up in rehab or jail."

"I can't understand Brian and Brittany's relationship," Brian's mother Carol says and turns to Brittany. "You fight all the time? Why are you guys still together? I think your relationship is making both of you sick."

Brittany stares at Carol, and shrugs. "I know, but we love each other. I need Brian," she says to Carol.

Kym asks Brittany, "Have you ever worried about Brian's using?"

"He gets really controlling when he uses cocaine. He starts being controlling and accuses me of cheating on him or hitting on other guys. I never do that, I love Brian!" Brittany says.

"Cocaine!" his parents say in unison. "When is he using cocaine? We checked him to deal with his alcohol abuse? How can he afford cocaine without a job?" his father, Ken asks.

"Oh my God, is he dealing to get the money?" Brian's mother asks. She looks like she's going to hyperventilate.

Kym intervenes, "Wait a minute. Let's everyone take a deep breath. I see that this has caught you by surprise. However, it's normal for people to try drugs when they are drinking a lot."

"Well drinking is one thing, but drugs?!" Carol says, "This is because of YOU. He NEVER took drugs before he met you!"

Carol spits at Brittany.

"Are you kidding? He gave me my first line!" Brittany says with a raised voice.

Kym steps in at this point, "Okay, okay ladies. This is a really emotional situation, and I want to remind you that what you have in common is your love for Brian. The enemy here is addiction, not each other."

She says to Carol, "It can be really hard to watch people we love make decisions that seem confusing, especially when we honestly believe we KNOW better. This brings me to my second point,

We might like the feeling of control.

"Sometimes we over give or enable ourselves to feel like we're somehow keeping control over a situation that feels out of control to us. For example, I sell my alcoholic son's truck while he's in rehab so he won't drive drunk."

"You mean like calling Lonnie's doctors and telling them about the pills to try to get them to stop giving them to her?" Jim says.

Kym smiles at him.

"I take Angie's son to school because I don't trust her to get him there on time. I'm afraid she will be too hung over, or still up on that meth stuff, so I just handle it," Carmen admits.

"I control J.P.'s trust fund money so he has to come to me and I can control what he spends it on. I'm afraid to let him have it. I'm afraid of what he'll do with it."

"That makes sense to me," Kym says. "The problem is that you become his banker and the target of manipulation instead of his grandmother, right?"

Lucille nods, with tears in her eyes. "I hate it when he calls and asks me for money, and gets mad at me. The problem is his parents were never there for him, and I've always felt so badly for him that I think I may have tried to make-up for their neglect by being overindulgent," she admits.

"I know Jeff thinks I call him during the day to check to see if he's sober. If I'm honest, I think that's true. I make up other reasons to call, but I like to hear the sound of his voice so I can see if he's been drinking," Jeff's wife, Sandy admits.

"What changes if he HAS been drinking?" Kym asks.

"Probably nothing. I just feel like I'm better prepared, does that make sense?" Sandy asks.

"Absolutely," Kym says. "We'll try to have some kind of predictability in an unpredictable situation. It makes us have the illusion we have some control!" she laughs.

Kym wants to address their fear of getting a call from the coroner. Every family of addicts and alcoholics dread the 3:00 am call from the police or the coroner, and will be frantic to prevent it. However, she sees Lonnie's daughters and makes the decision not to go there.

Kym turns to Lonnie's girls, Erica and Amber. "Erica, can you think of anything you may do to try to control or predict how your mom is going to react?"

Erica thinks a moment and looks at her Dad. "Hmmm, I know by her voice when she is going to remember what I tell her. I can tell she's only pretending to listen to me."

"That's a great point. The thing is, when people like your mom get addicted to pills or alcohol THEY can't even predict how they will be. Because they don't want to admit to themselves they're addicted they'll try to "fake normal," and she probably does want to listen to you. But she's had too many pills. Does that make sense?"

Erica nods. "If Amber and I tell her that we want her to stop taking pills will she stop?"

"I know she'll try to stop." Kym looks at the group.

"You can love someone very much and not be able to stop drinking and using drugs. It has nothing to do with love. It's a chemical change in your brain that makes you crave the drug so much that you are physically sick or unbearably anxious until you drink or use to calm down. It has nothing to do with love."

"I'm not sure I believe that," says Carmen. "I think if Angie really loved her son she'd stop taking drugs. She'd choose Jose instead of her friends." Carmen says heatedly. "If she loved me she wouldn't put me in an position where I am driving her son to school in heavy traffic, and paying her rent so Jose will have a roof over his head. "

"Is it possible that if you weren't driving Jose, Angie would have to? If you weren't paying her rent, she would have to?" Kym suggests.

"Yes, but what if she doesn't? Should my grandson have to suffer because she's irresponsible?" Carmen challenges.

"If Jose were to be physically in danger or at risk, you could call child protective services and they could place Jose with you while Angie gets the help she needs. That's what's happening right now, correct? You have Jose while Angie is in treatment?"

"She would never forgive me for doing something like that!" Carmen says.

"You bring me to my next point, Carmen," Kym continues.

We can't deal with the conflict.

"A lot of times our enabling is because we can't stand the conflict saying 'no' will create. We dread the tantrums, the pushing, the manipulation, or the cold shoulder where they disappear for long stretches of time. So we give in, step in, we tell ourselves, "It's not worth it," and just handle their business for them."

"Everything with Cathy is a battle" Cathy's father Bill says heavily. "Just this morning, we were almost here and she called to tell us there was a pair of jeans she wanted. We had already driven 20 minutes and were almost here. I wasn't willing to turn around, drive 20 minutes back, and then 30 minutes here. We would have been really late. She should have called us yesterday. She slammed the phone down, and I know she thinks we disappointed her on purpose," he says.

Kym nods. "Yes, I heard her end. It was a pretty hard conversation."

"All of our conversations are like that," Cathy's mother Karen says. "I keep hoping we'll find something that will work for her, something that will click. I honestly think she hates us," Karen says tearfully.

"I am hoping to meet with you as a family later," Kym says sympathetically. "I know you can use some help bridging the tension between you."

Karen and Bill smiled at Kym gratefully.

"I get tired of how defensive Jeff can be, so sometimes I just let things go rather than confront his behavior. Then it adds up and at some point I blow up," Sandy admits.

Kym turns and writes on the board,

What should we do?

"Let's define love separately from keeping people from experiencing the natural consequences of their decisions. It is not loving to deprive someone of the opportunity to grow. Sometimes growing means your knees get scraped up.

You need to get support for yourselves while you learn to allow the people you love the dignity of their decisions. I brought you all Al-anon meeting lists. This is the Twelve Step group for family and friends of alcoholics and addicts whose lives have been affected by the drinking and using of their loved ones. There is also Nar-anon for families of drug addicts. Some churches offer 'celebrate recovery' support groups for codependents. We'll talk about that another time. Addiction and alcoholism is bigger than you, you won't outsmart it, outthink it, fix it. You need help to figure out how and when to set boundaries. I want you to know that I know that this is a really hard disease, and I never underestimate it."

"Okay, we'll break now, and get together again in a few minutes and the clients will join us." Kym announced.

Kym could feel the tension in her neck from the interaction between Carol and Brittany, and decided to call Janet to debrief.

"Girlfriend, it's gnarly here between Brittany and Brian's mother, Carol. LOTS of tension and seething resentment. Brittany broke the news Brian was using cocaine, which horrified his parents. I thought his mom was going to pass out!" Kym says.

"You mean because it was DRUGS," Janet exaggerates and laughs.

"Exactly! Our nice child couldn't be involved with people who do drugs. It must be the skanky girlfriend's fault!" Kym imitates Carol.

"Oh, wow, Kym. I am so sorry. No wonder the man doesn't have a voice of his own. He's probably dating the meth'ed up version of his mom."

"Isn't that what Freud said?" Kym grins

"That certainly explains a lot of the male choices in my life!" Janet laughs.

"Okay, I feel much better. I just needed to shake that off before going into the next group. Thanks for letting me vent," Kym says with a smile.

"Oh, vent to me any time. It's a treat to listen to someone else herding the cats." Janet laughs.

Kym could hear the chairs moving to enlarge the circle, and crossed over to join them. She feels the tension and awkwardness of the room, and decides to have everyone check in so she can see who belongs to whom. During the check in it was obvious that Cathy was choosing not to sit with her parents, and Kym decided to lay the groundwork for ongoing conversation by helping them get in touch with feelings and the need the feeling indicates.

The Work Goes On

"Good morning. In multifamily group today, we're going to learn to connect an emotion with what we need in response to the feeling. This is important because in addiction, everyone gets really disconnected with what they might be feeling, either numbing out or feeling overwhelmed. If you can become clearer about what you might be feeling you will have much greater success in asking for and getting what you need. You can also lessen being reactive and asking for things that don't actually address the feeling you are having.

I'm going to break the group up into pairs, people who do not know each other, and give each pair one photo copy of the worksheet. For each feeling there is an associated need. For example if you feel angry the need is to be heard. The object of this is to have you fill in as many feelings and needs as you can. You don't have to complete all eight. Just as many as your team can come up with."

"So, team up right now with someone next to you." Kym asks them. She watches them awkwardly connect with each other, and she was glad that everyone had to be with someone other than a family member because it made the tension between family members seem less obvious (aka, Cathy not sitting with her parents or J.P. pouting. It also gives the group a chance to meet someone new.

The level of sound in the room begins to rise as they introduce themselves to each other and begin working to compile their lists. Kym walks around the circle listening and giving hints when pairs seemed to be stuck.

Feeling & Needs List	
Feelings	**Needs**
1. Angry	1. To be heard
2. Lonely	2. Want to talk to someone
3.	3.
4.	4.

Kym was glad to see Angie paired with 15 year old Erica, and Lucille with 13 year old Amber. The girls seemed to be fine, much to Kym's relief.

The Work Goes On

J.P. was working with Lonnie's husband, Jim and Cathy's mother managed to work with Lonnie. Kym is always comforted by how the families of addiction always seem to recognize each other – *"It's a shared language,"* she thinks. *"That's probably why I'm so comfortable with them."* When she sees most of the pairs coming close to finishing she gives them five more minutes to finish up and then get back in the circle to share their answers.

This is the interesting part, because there is NO right answer, and people may come up with descriptions she would not have predicted.

"So, what did you guys come up with?" Kym asks as she stands by the white board.

"We came up with something different for angry," Donna says. "We said we wanted to object when something was unfair."

"That's a good point," Kym agrees. "If we didn't have objection we wouldn't have women's rights, low cost housing, or unions," she notes.

"We said frustrated and that we wanted to resolve the issue that was frustrating us," Jim says.

Kym writes this on the board. "Can you think of a time when you were frustrated and did resolve the issue? How did it feel?" she asked him.

"Yeah, I was frustrated with Lonnie checking out on her pills, and feel more hopeful now that she checked in for treatment. She did something about it."

"Great," Kym smiles. Lonnie smiles also.

"We said scared, and we wanted a hug," says Erica.

"We said confused and we wanted honesty," says Jeff.

The group continues to share their feelings and needs, and Kym could feel the energy in the room lightening. *"It's team work,"* she thinks to herself.

"You've all done a really good job. Does anyone notice that it feels differently in the room right now than when we started?" she asks the group.

Everyone thinks a moment.

Alan says, "I think it was cool to work on something with another person, and there was no way to be wrong."

"I think the key is working together," Kym agrees. "In addiction it is easy to become adversarial, and see each other as the problem rather than the disease as the problem. Rather than teaming up against the disease, we attack each other. I encourage you to use your time together during visitation to address problems in your relationships from a "we" perspective. How are "we" going to solve this issue?"

"Before we close I want to turn our attention to the coin ceremony for Tony." Tony's sister has come today and Kym invites her to start the ceremony. "We each take this coin and put positive energy into it, expressing both our hopes and concerns for Tony. Then he takes he coin with him into his next phase of recovery.

Tony's sister, Tina takes the coin and holds it. "Tony, I was so relieved when you agreed to come here. I've worried about your health, and you've seemed tired and unhappy for a long time. In the last month, you have a spark in your eye, and your sense of humor has come back." Tina has tears in her eyes. "I missed you and I am so happy to have the old Tony back. It's just the two of us now. I love you," she smiles at him.

Tony looks genuinely touched. Each person takes a turn wishing him well in his sobriety or appreciating something he offered while there.

The group ends with the Serenity Prayer and the group disperses to get some lunch and visit. Kym has arranged to meet with Cathy and her parents after lunch, so heads back to the office to chart the group and eat her own meal.

Jesse was part of the coin ceremony and follows Kym back to the office, which is nice for her so she can debrief.

The Work Goes On

"You were your usual awesome self," he says with a grin

Kym bows her head slightly, "Well, thank you very much," she says in a really bad Elvis imitation which makes Jesse laugh.

"Honestly, this was tough today, and I still have some hard conversations ahead of me." She starts to unwrap her sandwich and takes a bite, "I need some fuel," she mumbles with her mouth full.

"What's your plan with the prickly Cathy and her parents?"

"Well, I laid the foundation by discussing teamwork and joint problem solving, so I plan to continue that theme with them. The problem is there's such broken trust, so I'm not sure how much I have to work with. For relationships to heal you have to believe that people didn't hurt you intentionally, so it would be safe to let down your guard. If you believe it IS intentional then it would be nuts to let down your guard. See?"

"Yeah, that makes sense. You have to believe that deep down they really still care about you and the relationship."

"Exactly,' Kym says.

"Do you think J.P. really cares about his Grandmother? He's such a user." Jesse asks

"Hmmmm, I don't know what he's capable of. I know he knows he needs her, which to him might be the same as love. She's been a stable presence even if enabling."

"Was it weird having kids in there?" Jesse wondered.

"Only in that I would've addressed the fear of death most families of addicts have in this morning's session, but I'm not sure what and how much they know and I didn't want to freak them out. They're nice children. Lonnie and Jim have done something right, pills and all."

"Well I better get out there and see how everyone's doing," Jesse says. "I just wanted to check-in"

"I appreciate it. It helps," Kym says as she turns to the computer to start to make her chart entries from group. At the same time she opens an NPR window and listens to talk radio to keep her company.

As she is finishing her last notes, there is a knock on the door and Cathy and her parents have arrived.

Cathy

Cathy looks a little less "fluffy tailed," and her mother, Karen, looks less brittle.

"Welcome, you have excellent timing!" Kym smiles, and invites everyone to take a seat.

"Bill and Karen, I understand from Cathy that you felt she needed to check into residential treatment. The alternative was to live with her grandparents. I gather that you are worried about the people in her life if you feel that separating her is the solution?" Kym asks.

"I have been worried to death about the choices I see her making," Karen says.

"You don't like anything about me! My hair, my make-up, my friends! That's why you didn't bring my jeans. You want to control what I wear so I meet YOUR standards," Cathy accuses.

"I know you believe that I was being controlling when I told your mother this morning I wouldn't turn the car around," Bill says to Cathy, "But that's just not reasonable!"

Kym intervenes. "How long have you been in this kind of power struggle with your daughter?' Kym asks Bill.

"Adopted daughter," Cathy barks which makes her mother wince.

Bill sighs. "I honestly don't know. For some reason Cathy thinks it matters to us that she is adopted - like we would love her more if she was ours by blood."

"I think you would," Cathy says. "Then I would look more like you, sound more like you, be similar to you. Instead I am so different in the things I like, the way I think that I make you uncomfortable."

"It's true that I don't understand you sometimes, Cathy. And the drug use scares me. But that would be true even if you weren't adopted," Karen points out.

"What are the choices you are seeing that worry you?" Kym asks Karen.

"She's right, I'm worried about her friends, what she's reading, the music she listens to. It is all so dark, and it seems so angry to me. I'm scared she's going to get hurt or raped at one of the parties she goes to."

Cathy rolls her eyes, "As if. . ."

"Actually Cathy, that's not insane. Some statistics indicate that over 80% of alcoholic and addicted women have experienced physical and sexual abuse. Date rape happens, especially when everyone's loaded," Kym says

Cathy shrugs, "I can handle myself."

Kym says, "I'm sure you can, when you're not loaded. You're actually really smart and have good street smart skills. But all of us, loaded, lose our edge."

"I want to know how I can reach you, Cathy," Bill says. "I hate fighting with you all the time. Everything's a battle."

"It's because I feel like you're always trying to change me!" Cathy says

Bill nods, "I can see that. I have trouble saying what I'm feeling. I tend to tell you more than ask you. Your mom complains about that all the time," he smiles. Karen nods.

"I worry because you're so angry," Karen said. "I sometimes feel like you're trying to force us to send you away. I almost feel like you're testing to see how much we can take until we send you away."

"Well, you DO send me away to my grandparents."

"I know we have. Sometimes it's because the fighting is so exhausting we feel like we all need a break. But we're always glad to see you when you get home. We're never thinking that we will never see you." Karen says.

Cathy sits quietly, unusually still.

"Cathy, what do you think about what your mom is saying about testing them to see if they will get rid of you? Anything to that?" Kym asks gently.

"I never thought about it like that. I don't think I do it on purpose."

"No, I don't think so either," says Kym. "But it's not unusual for adopted kids to worry at some level about being abandoned again, and to watch for signs that it's going to happen. Sometimes provoking it to happen at least ends the waiting and watching for it, does that make sense?"

Cathy nods, "Yeah."

"I would suggest that you three spend some time during this visitation period getting to know each other – your interests, things you think about, places you would like to travel, etc. I mean, like you're just people. You need to have some time that's less intense. Does that make sense?" Kym asks

They all nod, and head out of the office to the backyard where Cathy can smoke.

Kym sits back in her chair and breathes for a minute. *"I guess that went as well as it could have,"* she thinks. *"I will freak out if my son is that angry at her age."*

She takes a few minutes and makes a note in Cathy's chart and then goes to the main area to track down Brian, Brittany, and his parents. They're having a stilted conversation, and Brittany appears physically restless.

"Hello," Kym calls out as she comes closer. "I'm hoping this is a good time to meet" Kym offers.

Ken, Brian's father looks gratefully at Kym, "I think this would be a great time. Who do you want to see? All of us?" he asks.

"I think I would like to see Brian and the two of you first, and then Brian and Brittany. Brittany would you mind waiting? I promise it won't be too long," Kym asks her.

"It's okay," she mumbled, and gets out her cell phone to play Candy Crush.

Brian

Once the family was settled, Kym asked them, "How is your visit going?"

"How come you didn't bring Brittany in? I hate her sitting alone out there," Brian asks anxiously.

"I understand that you worry about Brittany a fair amount," Kym comments.

"That girl is ruining his life!" Carol exclaims. "He's addicted because of her," Carol says tearfully.

"That's not true! I started smoking pot and drinking in high school. You guys just never paid attention, all you cared about was my grades. As long as I was doing okay, you didn't ask any questions." Brian says.

Ken leans forward. "Brian, is it true that you were using cocaine?"

"Yeah, I used lots of things over the last few years. What's the big deal? Everyone my age parties."

"You know, Brian, people your age DO party. They also have often finished school, have a job, and are looking toward living independently," Kym observes. "The concern is that you've fallen behind, for some reason, and it's possible that alcohol and drugs have played a role in keeping you stuck," she says gently.

Brian was quiet. "I've had really bad luck... nothing ever seems to work out for me."

"Brian we just want to help you get back on track," Ken says. "I'll admit drugs scare me a little, I don't know anything we can do about them. But nonetheless, the goal is to do whatever it takes."

Brain sighs. "I know you must be really disappointed in me."

"Are you disappointed in you?" Kym asks him.

Brian nods. "I guess so. It seems weird that I'm already 25. I don't know how that happened," he says.

"I'm afraid he can't get better if he dates that girl," Carol worries.

"Carol, Brian is 25 years old, and will choose the person he dates. I strongly encourage you to focus on how you're going heal as a family." Kym says.

Carol sat still. "You mean pick my battles?"

"I mean focus on what you CAN control. Here, let me give you this Al-Anon schedule. There are meetings for parents of addicts and alcoholics, and I think it might be helpful for you to talk to other parents."

"What I'd like to do right now is meet with Brian and Brittany. You guys did great for a first session!" Kym smiles as Carol and Ken wander out to the kitchen. Brian goes and returns with Brittany in tow.

"Hi Brittany, thanks for your patience," Kym welcomes her. As the two are getting settled, Kym notices that Brittany seems to be sweating. Her movements seem a little jerky, actually and Kym catches Brian watching Brittany out of the corner of his eye.

"So, I wanted to talk to you about how Brian's sobriety might affect your relationship. I know you guys have partied together, so I'm wondering if you've thought about how things might change?" Kym asks.

"I don't think it's a problem when Brian drinks. He's only a problem when he uses coke. If he stops doing lines I think we'll be okay," Brittany says.

"I'm not sure I'm even an addict, yet" Brian tells Kym. "You made a good point that my life seems to have stalled, and maybe I should cut back. But I'm not sure I'm really an addict."

"Only you really know, and you're in a place where you are going to get a lot of information to help you figure it out." While Kym is speaking she's watching Brittany pick compulsively at her fingernails.

"Brittany, are you okay?" Kym asks.

"Why," Brittany snaps, "What?"

"You seem a little agitated. I have to ask you if you've taken something since you've been here at the center?"

"Oh, seriously?! You sound like his bitch mother," Brittany exclaims.

"It's not cool to accuse her like that," Brain says defensively.

"I know this is uncomfortable for both of you. My job is to keep the treatment center a safe place, and if I think someone may be using drugs or alcohol while they're here I need to ask them to test." Kym explains. "So, I'm asking you to take a drug test to stay for the remainder of the visit," Kym asks.

Brittany stares at Brian, "Seriously?" She turns to Brian," Are you going to let her pick on me? You didn't stand up for me with your mom in group either!" she accuses.

"Brittany, I am so, so sorry, baby." Brian reassures her. "I think you should leave her alone. She's not going to pee for you," he insists to Kym.

"Brittany, if you don't test for me, I'll have to ask you to leave." Kym states.

"Screw you, lady. I don't need this shit! I'm outa here," she yells as she heads out of the room.

Brian looks furiously at Kym, "Thanks a lot. Now she'll never come back!" he says as he storms after Brittany.

Kym gets up to follow them and sees Brian and Brittany leaving out the front door, followed by his confused parents. Jesse hears the commotion and comes out to the front from the group room. "What's up? Are you okay?" he asks Kym. She nods and says, "You need to go outside and check on Brian. I asked Brittany to test and they both bounced."

Jesse opened the front door to see Brian arguing with his parents and Brittany seated in the back seat.

"I'm coming with you," he hears Brian say to his father

"No you're not, son. You agreed to be here, and you need to finish what you started. We can come back next Saturday and try it again."

"You won't bring Brittany!" Brain worries.

"We'll bring her if she wants to come," Ken says as he gets behind the wheel.

Carol is sitting like a stone in the passenger seat, saying nothing. She can't look at Brian or Brittany.

Jesse goes out to the driveway to support Brian. "Hey, bro, let it go for now. Nothing good's gonna come from this."

Brian's dad pulls out of the driveway. "I'll call you Brittany," Brian promises as he watches them drive away.

Jesse puts his hand on Brian's shoulder, which Brian shakes off as he stomps back into the center. "

Jesse sticks his head in the office and says to Kym, "Would you call Sarah and ask her to start her shift earlier? I need her help."

"Don't we have to talk to Janet first?"

"I'll handle that part. You can just call Sarah," he says as he heads back to find Brian.

Kym places the call. Sarah's happy to come in and she's on her way.

Kym takes a deep breath, reviewing the scene with Brittany and wondering if she could have handled it any differently. She opens the incident report folder and starts typing hoping that her thoughts will get clearer as she writes.

At 2:10 Family counselor was meeting with Brian and his S.O. The S.O. had been alone in the center waiting for the meeting while the counselor met with Brian and his parents. During the meeting with the couple, the S.O. appeared to be sweating, picking obsessively at her fingers, and demonstrating jerky movements. She appeared to be under the influence. Counselor asked her to test in order to remain in the facility. S.O. refused to test, Brian became agitated, and as the S.O. and parents left the facility he was in the driveway arguing with Dad about leaving with them. Dad refused. Jesse went to support Brian in the driveway and asked him to return to the facility. He is meeting with him at this point in time.

Kym ended her narrative at that point, and decided to wait for further information from Jesse. In the meantime, she realized that Lonnie and Jim were still waiting to meet with her, so she needed to compartmentalize and refocus. She went to the main area and asked them to join her, leaving the 2 girls playing hearts with Donna, Angie and Carmen.

Lonnie

Is Brian okay?" Lonnie asks anxiously

"I am sure he'll be fine, Jesse will talk with him. I'm hoping you had a good visit and I'm wondering how it was with the girls, and if you had a chance to talk to them about why you're here, answer questions, etc."

Lonnie nodded, "I almost lost it when they asked me if I was going to stop taking pills," she says as tears flood her eyes.

Jim took her hand.

"What did you tell them?" Kym asks gently

"I said that I didn't realize how much they had been affected, and that I was sorry. I really am," she says as tears roll down her cheeks. "I was saving up my emotion until we got in here. I didn't want them to see me cry."

"What's it been like at home?" Kym asks Jim.

He sighs. "It's been hard juggling my work schedule with school pick up. I've been able to ask other parents sometimes which has helped. Then I need to fix dinner and help them with homework. Honestly, I had no idea how much Lonnie does because she just makes it happen."

"Like the laundry fairy?' she giggles through her tears.

"Exactly."

And he turns to Lonnie. "Lonnie, I can't do this without you. I know I've been mad at you, judgmental. But I'm scared. I can't be a single parent. I can't handle it if you get arrested again or God forbid, die." Jim says with a tight throat.

Kym sits patiently as Jim collects himself. "I guess I was saving that, too."

"They're telling me here that my pill abuse is a disease. I have a hard time with that, and I really want to blame the doctors. But every time I do that, Janet brings it back to my choices and the disease." Lonnie says.

"I don't really understand the disease part yet, either," Jim admits. "But I am starting to get that you can't handle it by yourself."

"That means there's no way YOU could have controlled it, either." Kym interjects.

Jim nods. "I felt so powerless."

"Because you were," Kym agrees. "You are both in the right place. Jim, you have a chance to go to Al-Anon and figure out how you're going to take care of yourself while Lonnie gets the help she needs. There is also Al-a-teen for the girls if they want to talk more about the addiction and how there's nothing they could do either."

Lonnie and Jim leave the room holding hands, which is comforting to Kym. *"What a hard day,"* she thinks.

Sarah enters the office as Jim and Lonnie rejoin the hearts game.

"Cute girls," Sarah notes as she puts her purse away.

"Indeed they are," Kym affirms. "It has been a grueling day, and I'm grateful to see you. I know Jesse needs you. We had a blow up with Brian when I asked his girlfriend to take a UA test. She was looking spun to me. It didn't go well, and Jesse's talking him out of the tree right now."

"Okay, I'll go check on the rest of the house, and see what everyone else is doing," she says as she takes off.

Kym sits still for a minute and picks up the phone.

"Hey, can I bother you?" Kym asks

"Hey yourself! You're never a bother" Janet laughs. 'You're tearing me away from NCIS, but I'll cope!"

"Well, I want to read my incident report to you. I tried to test Brian's girlfriend and it blew up. I want you to tell me if I missed anything, okay?"

"Oh, yeah, Jesse called about that. Is Sarah there?"

"She is. Here goes:

At 2:10 Family counselor was meeting with Brian and his S.O. The S.O. had been alone in the center waiting for the meeting while the counselor met with Brian and his parents. During the meeting with the couple, the S.O. appeared to be sweating, picking obsessively at her fingers, and demonstrating jerky movements. She appeared to be under the influence. Counselor asked her to test in order to remain in the facility. S.O. refused to test, Brian became agitated, and as the S.O. and parents left the facility he was in the driveway arguing with Dad about leaving with them. Dad refused. Jesse went to support Brian in the driveway and asked him to return to the facility. He is meeting with him at this point in time."

"It sounds pretty clear to me. What's bothering you about it?"

"I was predisposed to think of her as loaded because we called her his 'meth girlfriend.' In fact, I was calling her that when I was watching the family get out of the car, and so I'm afraid I may have created chaos for no reason," Kym explained.

"Oh, I get it. We shouldn't have done that. It creates distance between us and the clients to call them by their drug of choice. I'll mention that at staff meeting. But from what you read me, it seemed pretty clear that you would have to test her based on her behavior. So, I think both are true – sometimes stereotypes exist because they are the truth. You're absolved from any counter-transference issue, my friend."

Kym breathes a sigh of relief. "Thanks so much. On the other hand, we still have a mess to clean up. Brian is one anxious cat, and I don't know if he can hang in there with it ending on such a bad note."

"You're right, and the CD techs are going to have to watch him carefully. I think I'll meet them at the outside meeting tomorrow so I can help," Janet thought out loud.

"Well, other than that the sessions were tough, but manageable. Cathy and her parents have a long way to go. My heart goes out to them."

"I'm sure you made a good start. You did great, Kym. Try not to second guess yourself."

"Thanks, Janet. I've earned my shekels today!"

As Kym is gathering her things, Jesse appears which reminds her that she needs to complete her incident report.

"So, how's Brian doing? I wanted to add his current state to my incident report," Kym says.

"He's a little less agitated now that the families have left and they have phone time. He's left a couple of messages for Brittany, and he'll feel better once he hears from her. That guy is really lost in her. It's hard to tell if cocaine or Brittany is his drug of choice."

"I would guess Brittany," says Kym, "based on his mother's coldness. I can picture her being very conditional and stingy with approval, a great set-up to get an unreliable girlfriend he chases around trying to get her to love him."

"Ouch" smiles Jesse. "You've been reading my diary."

"Boy I hope not," Kym laughs. "If so you need to run, run, run to therapy my friend!"

Jesse just nods. "Okey Dokey."

Jesse wasn't kidding, actually. When he has relapsed in the past it was always over a relationship. He seems to have radar for women who disappear or change the rules on a regular basis and keep him unsettled. It's always exciting; the chemistry is great at first. Then the craziness sets in and he spends more and more time tracking her down, trying to stabilize her crisis. . . and he loses himself in the process. That's why his sponsor has him on a dating "time out" while he shores up his recovery. He almost lost his recovery 3 months ago, but fortunately his sponsor saw the train coming and was able to pull him off the tracks in time. It really scared Jesse, and he is wondering if Kym is right. This issue is bigger than the steps and he may need to get professional help.

Kym adds a couple of final sentences to her incident report and cc's Janet and the Clinical Director.

Sarah pops her head in. "Everyone seems pretty mellow, even J.P which worries me a little. I always wonder what that guy's up to, you know what I mean?" she asks Jesse.

"You're wise to think that, grasshopper," he says in his best Asian martial arts voice.

Sarah giggled. "Who's coming from H&I (Hospitals and Institutions) for the A.A. meeting tonight?"

Jesse checks the calendar. "It looks like it's Zack. I love that guy!"

he says enthusiastically. "The house is about to get some energy, Sarah."

"Jorge is scheduled to replace you tonight, so I'm sure all will be well. I'll keep an eye on Brian, and fill Jorge in." Sarah says

"I've put everything in the log as well," Kym interjects. "It's been a long day and I'm ready to pick up my boy, put on some sweats, and order a pizza."

Kym is always anxious picking up Andy from visitation with his Dad. She's never sure whether or not his dad will have been manic and the manic energy tends to make Andy's Asperger's even more pronounced. In the face of this stimulation Andy can get more rigid to compensate, which means he will not be flexible for a few hours after they get home. Everything becomes a negotiation. She feels a flash of anger at her ex because he can "choose" to not treat his Bipolar illness, and everyone else simply has to "manage" the fall out. She reminds herself of the powerlessness she talked about all day, and sends up a brief prayer that Andy is okay.

A.A. Meeting

The H&I speaker, Zack, arrives at 6:15, and Sarah is helping to set up the group room for the meeting. Jorge greets Zack with a recovery shoulder bump, and takes him into the group room. Zack spots J.P., who he saw at another H&I meeting at the correctional facility, and goes over to say "Hi." Zack has a heart for incarcerated folks, having been one himself.

Because it's an in-house meeting, the meeting format is shifted a little, though it is set up to be a full meeting experience. One of the residents will function as the secretary and follow the format, which is an opening and some readings. No one reads the secretary report or seventh tradition. Tonight's secretary will be Alan, who reads from the script:

1. Good Evening ladies and gentlemen. This is the Saturday H&I meeting of Alcoholics Anonymous. My name is Alan and I'm an alcoholic and your Secretary.

2. Let us open the meeting with a moment of silence to do with

as you wish followed by the Serenity Prayer:

God,
Grant me the serenity to accept the things I cannot change,
Courage to change the things I can, and
Wisdom to know the difference.

3. Alcoholics Anonymous is a fellowship of men and women who share their experience, strength and hope with each other that they may solve their common problem and help others to recover from alcoholism.

    The only requirement for membership is a desire to stop drinking. There are no dues or fees for AA membership; we are self-supporting through our own contributions. AA is not allied with any sect, denomination, politics, organization or institution; does not wish to engage in any controversy; neither endorses nor opposes any causes.

    Our primary purpose is to stay sober and help other alcoholics to achieve sobriety.

4. Lonnie will now read "How it Works" from Chapter 5 of the A.A. Big Book.

    Jeff will now read The Twelve Steps
    Donna will now read the Twelve Traditions

5. Will any new members to introduce themselves by their first name only--a new member is anyone who has a desire to stop drinking and is within their first thirty days in A.A.

6. Tonight our speaker will be Zack, who will share his experience, strength and hope and then we will open the meeting for sharing.

Zack is high energy and quickly begins with how it was, and moves to how it is now and how he uses the program to stay clean even though he has 6 years. He announces he will remain after the meeting for a while if anyone needs to talk, and clients have an opportunity to share. This is important practice for new people who have a chance to learn meeting format and culture.

Many people in recovery have never been listened to, and the lack of feedback allows them the space to hear themselves without worrying about another person's response. Lack of cross-talk can be really freeing.

The group was chatty after the meeting, infected with Zack's energy and humor, and Sarah thinks to herself that this was the perfect person to bring the message. She loves A.A., and was glad it was an A.A. meeting tonight instead of N.A.

Sarah has been working a strong A.A. program for a number of years, as well as Al-anon. Al-anon is much harder for her since it's all about relationships, people-pleasing and control which are hard issues for her to get a hold of. Even though she was introduced to the program through her Mother's sobriety when she was in high school, she gets down on herself that she hasn't "mastered" serenity all the time. Marriage and sharing control with her husband is hard for her and she finds herself withholding information and being secretive unnecessarily. It's almost as though she's afraid to let him get in a position to really "mess" with her. Her sponsor has pointed out that this strategy of self-protection could CAUSE the negative outcome she's most afraid of, yet she can't seem to stop herself sometimes. "I'm a work in progress" she tells herself in her more gentle moments. In her harsher moments she tells herself, "You are seriously f**ked up. You are lucky anyone would marry you at all!"

Sarah shakes off her thoughts and makes the rounds to check in with clients, make sure they're doing their chores, and takes the opportunity to play cards with them or watch T.V. Brian is in his room unless he's outside smoking. He still hasn't heard from Brittany and he's pacing like a caged lion.

Jorge steps outside to have a cigarette with Brian.

"Hey, man. How you holding up? You look a little jumpy."

"She hasn't called. When she doesn't call she's usually using, so I'm worried. I don't know who she's with, how she's getting home. I am f**king stressed out!" Brian says.

Jorge nods. "I can see why. Silence is always harder for me. I'd rather have you yell at me than say nothing."

"Exactly! I just need to know she's okay after the blow up today. Man, she was so mad at me. She thinks I should have stood up to Kym and my mom about her. I feel like shit."

"Can I ask you something?" Jorge says.

"Yeah."

"Do you think she might have been on one – maybe DID use when you were in session with your folks?"

Brian is quiet.

"Cause if you think she did, it would have been harder to stand up for her, you know what I mean?"

"She probably did. Being with my mom stresses her out. We shouldn't have left her alone," Brian admits.

"The thing is, I hear YOU taking responsibility for her using when she was here. My guess is you take on a lot of her responsibilities."

"You mean like driving her to DUI? I'm just helping."

"Yeah. And I also would guess you help protect her from her decisions in other ways, when you can."

"That's what you do when you love someone, man. You have their back!" Brian says.

"I'm just saying that sometimes people need to have the natural consequences of what they do in order to learn and grow. Maybe your girlfriend needed a little reality testing – that she's not fooling anyone. When we're using we always think no one can tell. You probably thought you were fooling your parents."

"Well they DIDN'T notice for a long time. As long as my grades were okay they never said anything."

"Do you kind of wish they HAD noticed? Maybe your disease wouldn't have progressed and your life wouldn't be sidetracked like it is," Jorge wondered.

Brian looked thoughtful. 'I never thought about it that way."

"Sometimes we need feedback to make a course correction, you know what I mean?"

Brian nodded.

"I gotta go back inside," Jorge says. "It's been cool talking to you."

The clients are starting to head to their rooms when Carl arrived for the night shift. He greets Sarah and Jorge, and goes into the office to read the log book and catch up. He's always amazed how much can jump off in just 24 hours.

The Work Goes On

SUNDAY

2:00 a.m. Janet's phone rings. She's confused at first, thinking it's the alarm, then sleepily answers the phone, "Yeah?"

"Janet, it's Carl. I'm sorry to wake you."

"What time is it?"

"It's a little after 2:00. I just finished my rounds and Brian's not in his room."

"Hmmmm. Are his clothes in the closet?"

"Yeah, except for his jacket."

"How was he at bedtime?"

"He was still spinning because his girl hadn't called. We talked during his last cigarette break, and we had a plan to try to reach her in the morning."

"Honestly, I'm not surprised he left. Go ahead and log it, including the conversation. Good job, Carl. Thanks for calling. I'll call the Clinical Director at a more civilized time."

"Okay, boss."

7:30 a.m. Jesse and Keisha arrive for shift change to relieve Carl. Keisha hears the clients stirring, so goes to check on them while Carol debriefs Jesse.

"So, everything is there but his jacket?" Jesse asks.

"I didn't do a heavy search because I didn't want to wake Jeff up any more than I already had. But that's all that was obviously missing," Carl reports.

"Okay. I'm not surprised, especially if he never heard back from Brittany. Thanks a lot, Carl."

"No problem, boss. I'm going home to crash."

The Work Goes On

Jesse finished reading the rest of the log and went out to the kitchen for a cup of coffee. Jeff was toasting a bagel.

"Good morning, bro." Sorry about the commotion last night."

"No problem. I didn't hear Brian leave. Just Carl checking his closet. I hope he's okay," he says with a yawn.

"Well I guess his girlfriend never called."

"Yeah, he was pretty stressed out."

Clients are beginning to come into the kitchen, sleepily seeking coffee.

"Hey, there's no sugar!" Alan exclaims as he roots around the cabinet.

"There has to be, the chef just went shopping this week," Jesse says as he begins opening cabinets. "Hmmmm. The cook also bought cans of fruit cocktail . . . we probably have ketchup and bread," Jesse says.

"Okay, that sounds disgusting. What are you talking about?" Keisha asks him as she walks into the kitchen with Donna.

Jesse starts to shake his head. "I bet there's some pruno (prison alcohol) heating up somewhere! It's good we're doing double scrub today so I can find it." Jesse laughs.

Just then Alicia hurries into the kitchen. "Jesse, someone's really sick in the hall bathroom. I can hear them throwing up over and over again!"

"Shit. It's ready to drink," Jesse calls as he races down the hall. He opens the bathroom door to see Jason bent over the bowl, wracked with stomach spasms.

"Jason, dude, what have you been drinking?"

Jason bends over and vomits violently. Jesse hears vomiting in the bathroom next to J.P.'s room.

"Shit, Keisha call an ambulance. We need to check these guys

The Work Goes On

out," he calls down the hall. "NO sirens!" he yells.

Keisha dials 911 and goes into the bathroom with Jason who looks very, very pale and is shaking. She grabs a cold wash cloth and starts to mop his face, when he turns to vomit some more. Keisha has a strong vomit reflex herself, so begins to feel her own stomach heaving in response, so she runs out of the room to take a few breaths while he is throwing up.

Donna is posted up at the front window and yells, "They're here," and opens the door for the EMT's who rush down the hall where she directs them.

Keisha gratefully steps aside to allow the EMT to take a look at Jason while she takes the other one to J.P.'s bathroom, where he's still doubled over the toilet having stomach spasms. Then she gathers the rest of the clients in the kitchen/dining area to have breakfast and wait out of the way.

The EMTs put Jason on a gurney due to severe dehydration and possible stomach bleeding. J.P. was going to be okay but needed bed rest for at least 24 hours. The remainder of the pruno was still in the plastic bag it had been fermenting in, looking like the vomit it triggered.

Jesse took the bag, and walked the EMTs out. He returned to the dining area to check in with the clients.

"Okay guys, that was an intense start to the day. How are ya doing?"

"What's wrong with them?" asks Alan.

"Well, it looks like J.P. made some homemade pruno, which is fermented fruit and mold, to make alcohol. Unfortunately the mold ingredient can make you really sick if you don't know what you're doing."

"So that's where all the sugar went?" Angie asks.

"Exactly. See, this is how far we'll go to change the way we feel. It's not about a high when you're drinking pruno, guys."

"What's wrong with Jason?" asks Lonnie. "Is he dehydrated?"

"Yeah, they are also worried about some stomach bleeding. This is serious stuff guys."

"What's going to happen now? Are they going to be kicked out?" Cathy wonders. "And where's Brian?"

"Brian chose to leave last night, probably because his girlfriend never called." Keisha explains.

"We're going to stick with our structure and start double scrub pretty soon. So, go ahead and get dressed and we'll begin in a little while." Jesse announces.

Jesse goes into the office to call Janet, and fill her in.

"Good morning sunshine."

"Well, sort of. I talked to Carl at 2:00, so I know about Brian."

"Old news, baby. The EMTs just left with Jason and J.P. is on bed rest for 24 hours after downing some homemade pruno,"

"Oh my God. Seriously? That stuff is gross, even when it's made right."

"Well, it wasn't. I have the rest of it in the office. You know, if J.P.'s making alcohol here, he's going to have to go, I think. I'm pretty sure that's going to be a deal breaker, especially after threatening Tony last week."

"You're probably right. We'll call his P.O. in the morning. In the meantime, he needs to lie in. I'll meet you at the outside meeting tonight so Keisha can stay at the center with him."

"Will you call the Clinical Director? He's going to be SO pissed," Jesse asks.

"I was about to call him about Brian, so your timing's great. Do you need anything?"

"No, we're good. We'll start double scrub in a few minutes. We were going to go to the park before the meeting, but I think we'll

The Work Goes On

skip that since Keisha needs to stay here with J.P."

"That sounds like a good call. Write it up for me, Jesse. I can't thank you enough for handling everything so well. We're so lucky to have you."

"Ah, thanks boss," he says in an imitation of Carl which makes Janet laugh as she hangs up. She dials the Clinical Director at home.

"Good morning, did I wake you?"

"No, I caught a 6 a.m. meeting. What's up – it can't be good if you're calling this early."

"Well it's been a little wild. Brian took off last night with just his jacket. Carl found him missing at the 2:00 check."

"Well at least Carl wasn't jacking off at your computer. Do we know why Brian took off?"

"Kym had requested his girlfriend test because she seemed loaded, and the girl stormed off and didn't return his calls all day. I think he couldn't stand it anymore and took off to find her."

"Shit. It's usually women that take us out."

"That so? The other thing is that J.P. apparently made some homemade pruno, resulting in Jason being transported to the hospital for dehydration and potential stomach bleeding. J.P is on bed rest for 24 hours. "

"God dammit, that little shit bird! I should've shipped him off earlier this week! Okay, we call his P.O. and leave a message today, and follow-up in the morning demanding that he come get the kid. Shit, that stuff is nasty!" the Clinical Director spouts. "How are the rest of the clients?"

"Jesse thinks it's given them something to think about. They'll be okay, but the park trip is out. Keisha needs to stay at the center with J.P."

"I'll call his P.O. Johnson myself, it'll be fun to talk to that prick," the Clinical Director barks.

"Well I don't want to cheat you!" Janet laughs.

"How do you want to follow-up with Jason at the hospital? Who's his emergency contact?"

"I expect his Mom. I'll have Jesse check his chart and call her."

"Okay. Never a dull moment, huh?"

"You got it, boss," Janet says imitating Carl. "Boss" always makes the Clinical Director wince.

The clients are pretty quiet during the double scrub, unusually cooperative. They chat amongst themselves, replaying family day and talking about Brian. After this kind of chaos, it is not unusual for clients to be quiet. In fact, the rest of the afternoon is pretty mellow, with limited push back about cancelling the park. It's interesting to watch the clients be on the receiving end of alcohol and drug created chaos. Groups should be interesting on Monday.

The Work Goes On

MONDAY

Janet decides to come to work a little early to check on J.P., and read the incident reports before women's group. She makes a cup of tea and some dry toast, and walks back to J.P.'s room.

The room is dark so she lifts the shade a few inches to let in the light, and gently calls to him as she pulls a chair up next to the bed.

"Hmmmmmm" he mumbles and pulls the pillow over his face. "J.P., I brought you some tea and toast. You need to get some liquids in you," Janet says quietly.

He moves the pillow from his face.

"How are you?" Janet asks

"I feel like shit, and my ribs hurt," he mumbles.

"Yea, I read that you were vomiting pretty hard. Have you ever made pruno before, or was this your first try?"

"I saw them do it in prison when I was there for a few months. It looked simple."

"What do you think now?"

"I guess it's not. What's going to happen to me now?"

"For now, you're going to continue to rest, and I am going to talk to the team."

"Where's Jason?"

"Jason's still at the hospital, they kept him overnight to pump him with fluids."

"F**k," he says as he rolls back toward the wall.

"J.P., I'm going to leave the toast and tea here, and hope that you'll at least sip a little and nibble some toast. I'll come back and check on you later," Janet says as she gets up to leave the room.

Back in the office Janet sips her coffee and reads the log, which was substantial in only two short days! Then she reviews and signs off on the incident reports the counselors have filed over the weekend. She'd brought a bag of sugar cubes for the morning coffee, knowing that the chef could go shopping later that day to restock so the clients would be content.

She decides to follow up with the Clinical Director about J.P.'s Parole Officer.

"Hey, did you leave a message this weekend for Officer Johnson or are you going to call him this morning?" Janet asks.

"I left a message for him with the Officer of the Day yesterday, and am just about to call him myself this morning. How's he feeling?" the Clinical Director inquires.

"He feels like crap still. I left him some tea and toast and told him to lie in for now. In a perfect world we would have the P.O. come during a class time so the client's will be in group. That's the least disruptive."

"I have the schedule in front of me. I'll ask for that consideration, but they come when they can."

"After he goes I'll have Jorge pack up his stuff and will call his grandmother to come and get his belongings."

"I'm sure it's not the first time she has taken care of his things. Did someone pack up for the other kid, Brian?"

"Keisha took care of it, and his dad came by and picked up Brian's things while the clients were at the outside meeting. So, it was a smooth transfer."

"Has the dad heard from him?"

"Not yet, but assumes he's staying with the girlfriend. It's a pretty good guess."

"Okay, I'll call Johnson. Thanks for pitching in over the weekend."

Ricardo walks in and Janet mouths, "Hi Dad" with a smile. He smiles back and holds up the pruno bag, "Que?" he mouths and pretends to shiver.

"You got it," Janet says into the phone.

Residential treatment centers are not locked facilities, and it not uncommon for clients to leave the facility, often in the middle of the night, even though they're free to leave at any point. There's a protocol for packing their things, notifying the emergency contact if there is one, and preparing the bed for the next resident. Client's belongings are held for no more than 30 days, then donated, or they're kept in the clothes closet for clients who need clothing.

Women's Group

The women are settling in as Janet enters the room, and they look at her with curiosity. They've had 24 hours to process the "drama" amongst themselves, so are interested in what will happen at the center next. One of the problems with "drama" is that it is highly distracting. Clients resist looking at themselves even on a good day, so if there's something external to speculate about, wonder about, focus on... they will choose to do so. Janet knew her main goal this morning was to direct them back to themselves and their personal issues.

"Good morning, ladies. You've had an eventful two days, I see. Sometimes when stuff is jumping off in the external world, we can lose track of our internal world. So our task this morning is to refocus on you and your own program. Does that make sense?" Janet began.

"I have no problem with that, because I've been thinking about my visit with my kids since Saturday. I keep remembering their faces, and wondering what they thought after they left. I've talked to them on the phone a couple of times, but so far they haven't said a whole lot." Lonnie says.

"What are you afraid they might be thinking?" Janet asks.

"I'm not really sure. That mommy's a freak, maybe? That I look okay so why aren't I home? I'm not sure what they took away from the groups. I appreciate you guys for treating them so well, though."

"I enjoyed them," Donna says. "I miss my nieces, and it was fun to interact with people their age. Honestly, I think they were fine. They seemed to be taking everything in, but didn't seem too freaked out."

"Were you freaked out?" Janet asks Lonnie.

"A little," Lonnie admits. "I was worried that they'd judge me."

"My guess is they were relieved to see how normal you looked," Janet offered.

"I thought my meeting with my parents was intense," Cathy jumps in. "It's so hard for us to have a conversation. Kym said she thought I might be pushing them away to see if they'll dump me like my bio mom did."

"What do you think about that theory?" Janet asks.

"I thought it was pretty far out at first, but I'm starting to see it a little as I think about it. It sort of makes sense."

"I know I wait all the time for my partners to dump me," says Donna. "And I'm not even adopted. So I can only guess what that could be like."

"My mom is really struggling with the disease thing," Angie says. "She really believes I wouldn't use meth if I loved Jose. Honestly, I wonder about that too, which is why I feel so guilty all the time."

"I can understand that," Janet says. "It's hard to wrap your head around having a disease that makes you DO things. It always looks like you are choosing."

"Well we are, sort of," says Cathy. "I choose to meet my dealer."

"Your frontal lobe part of your brain, the part that chooses and has impulse control, is 'off-line' when you use drugs and alcohol regularly. It is automatic behavior in response to craving. Your brain has changed which is why we see it as a disease." Janet explains.

"Do you think Brian's girlfriend Brittany really used drugs here in the center?" Lonnie asks Janet.

"I honestly don't know. I do know that when we're addicted, our craving makes us do things we would normally never do. Has that ever been true for you guys?"

"I know I've done LOTS of things I was embarrassed to hear about later," another resident Susan laughs.

"I can't believe the things that come out of my mouth!" Donna says.

"A lot of early recovery is coming to terms with the choices we made when our brain was off-line and learning to forgive ourselves and move on. It is not the easiest part," Janet says

"Especially if they won't let you forget," says Angie. Everyone nods.

Back in the office, Janet is curious about Ricardo's men's group because over the weekend he lost Tony, Brian, Jason, and J.P. is in bed.

"How did the guys do this morning? Your group was really hit hard over the weekend," Janet asks Jesse and Ricardo

"Tell me about it. It took a lot of work to get them to focus back on their own recovery. Obviously we need to talk about warning signs of relapse and what they are seeing in themselves."

"The women, God bless them, were able to focus on themselves quite well, actually. I think it's because we lost the guys, so they related a little less."

"J.P. is still in his room. I heard you check on him. I'll go see him later. Do we have an E.A.T. for his P.O.? I really hope the Clinical Director was able to emphasize the importance of coming during groups."

"He said he was going to, but there is only so much control he has."

"How did he take the pruno incident?" Ricardo asks

"About the way you would expect him to," Janet laughs. "He's handling the P.O. because he wants to, if that gives you any clue."

"I guess J.P. is lucky he's not over here right now jacking him up. He must be tempted."

"I think the fact that J.P. feels like crap physically takes away some of the impulse to come over and make him miserable. He's already miserable."

"Well, we'll have Jorge on alert so he can whisk the P.O. in and out when he arrives. J.P. knows the drill and isn't really himself, so it will go smoothly."

"Do you think the P.O. will use the handcuffs?"

"I think they have to in these situations."

"Sometimes a perp walk can be a good reminder to the clients in treatment who may need a little reality check."

"I know it will freak Lonnie out," Janet says.

"I imagine most of them will sympathize, and identify. I certainly will!" Ricardo laughs.

Community Group

While Jorge keeps an eye on the front of the building, Janet, Ricardo and Jesse meet with community group. The clients are assembled and do their check in. Janet opens the group for concerns and appreciations.

"I'm concerned that we didn't get to go to the park this weekend, and I'm feeling a little stir crazy. Is there something planned pretty soon?" Cathy asks.

The Work Goes On

"Yeah. I know things were pretty nuts, and I get why it changed, but I was really looking forward to a change in venue," adds Alan.

"I don't blame you," Jesse answers. "You guys were champs this weekend, and I appreciate your flexibility. When I meet with the Clinical Director in staffing today I will see what we can put together."

"How's Jason?" Jeff asks.

"That's a good question," Janet says. "I'm waiting for the hospital to give me a release time. I spoke with his mom who says he is feeling much better now that he has fluids. Hopefully you can ask him yourself sometime today."

"What's going to happen to the guys?" Donna wonders.

"I am not real sure," Janet says. "We still have to meet as a staff and make some decisions>"

"I think they've been punished enough by getting so sick," says Angie.

"It's not about punishment, Angie. It's about structure and how we operate," says Ricardo.

Angie looks annoyed.

The clients continue to check in with house issues, like chore scheduling and toilet paper needs and the group ends peacefully. Ricardo disappears to check on J.P. and Janet and Jesse return to the office.

"I always feel weird saying we haven't made a decision when I know damned well that the P.O. is coming," says Janet.

"I know, I feel the same way. But to say anything else would open the floor to discussion and debate. At least that's what my supervisor told me once," he smiles.

Janet giggles, "Smart supervisor."

"I hope we get some more guys soon, you are going to be overrun by estrogen!" Janet laughed.

"Well, it wouldn't be the first time I have been helpless in the face of the fairer sex," Jesse quips, which reminds him to call a therapist today like he promised his sponsor he would.

Ricardo returns to the office. "Hey guys. J.P.'s up and taking nourishment, as my grandmother used to say. He's feeling well enough to start defending himself."

"Jeez, I hope the P.O. appears soon. Otherwise, we're going to have to deal with the energetic version of him." Janet worries.

"I told him to stay in bed for now like the doctor ordered." Ricardo reassures Janet.

Psychoeducation

Ricardo and Jesse decide that Stress Management might be a good topic given the chaos over the weekend and pulls out **What is Stress?** from the curriculum. Ricardo starts by having the clients take a small test, and then will review a handout that describes stress and it's symptoms.

Take the Stress Test: Are You Stressed?

1. Do you feel tired all the time or have trouble sleeping?
2. Do you have a hard time relaxing or feel unable to relax?
3. Do you forget things all the time?
4. Are you frequently angry and tired at the end of the day?
5. Do you always feel under pressure?
6. Do you argue all the time, even about minor things?
7. Can you never find time for yourself?
8. Do you no longer want to socialize with others?
9. Do you lack patience and feel others are always wrong?
10. Do people often tell you that you seem tense or upset?

People in early recovery are always stressed, it is part of Post Acute Withdrawal for the first six months of sobriety. They can be over-reactive, have sleep problems, mood swings, poor concentration. It's part of the brain healing and the frontal lobe coming back on line. Stress is a major relapse trigger and important for the clients to be clear about.

Clinical Staffing

Janet is on the phone when the Clinical Director strides in and asks, "Johnson show up yet?"

"Not yet. I take it you spoke to him?" Janet says as she hangs up. "He never pays attention to what other people are doing," she thinks to herself. "It's like he starts a conversation in mid-sentence"

"Yeah, I did. He knew immediately who the kid is, and is happy to come get him like I predicted. He's going to try to come to match our schedule but he didn't promise. Is he up?"

"He's doing better, but I asked him to stay in bed. He'll probably get up for lunch though," Ricardo says.

"Hmmm. The more energy he gets the more agitated he may get,"

"Actually, he could just bounce," says Jesse.

"Well, he wouldn't be the first, now would he?" the Clinical Director jokes as he opens the log.

Jorge joins the group carrying a sandwich, soon Sarah and Carl arrive followed by Eddie, Kym and Keisha. Janet's looking forward to finding some time with Eddie to check in. She's worried about his mood change last week after Sarah was assigned to his shift with him.

Carl reaches over and picks up the pruno bag, "Oooo wheee, I haven't seen this in a long time! Who's the cook?"

"That would be our resident hard-ass, J.P." Ricardo answers.

"Whatever happened to having your friends stash a pint in the bushes like a respectable residential client?" Eddie joked.

"So that's why they offer to mow the lawn in the front all the time!" Sarah laughs.

"J.P.'s Parole officer should be coming by sometime today for him. After his threat to Tony last week, he has outstayed his welcome," Janet says. "The question on the table is what should Ricardo do with Jason?"

"Well, he's been really sick, so got an immediate consequence," Jesse points out.

"It's really hard to blame the guy when the alcohol is put in his room. Most addicts couldn't handle that kind of temptation. I know I couldn't have when I was in treatment," Jorge offers.

"On the other hand, pruno takes a while to make, so we don't know how long he knew about it. He may have had plenty of time to tell us about it," the Clinical Director says.

"So we're saying it makes a difference if he knew in advance or not?" Keisha asks.

"It has to do with the role of impulse control. If he didn't know and had the opportunity, it makes sense to let his illness be the lesson. If he knew all week, we can either exit him for putting the house at risk with J.P. or have him start his treatment program all over again." Janet explains.

"I've been working with Jason, and honestly he's pretty immature. This is his first time in treatment so either way, he wouldn't have handled himself well. For what it's worth, I think he should start over again. He needs more time to get stable," Ricardo observes.

"You know him best, Ricardo. Honestly, I agree with you based on my interactions with him," Janet agrees. "We'll talk to him when he's released and his mom brings him back. You'll have to include mom, because she'll need to pay for his extended stay," she says to the Clinical Director.

"No problem."

"How did Brian's dad handle it when he came to get Brian's things?" Janet asks Keisha.

"He was quiet and sad. I felt really bad for him because he feels so out of control. I reminded him about Al-anon, I really hope he goes."

"It was a tough family session," Kym offered. "Mom really blames everything on Brittany, and it sounds like Brittany makes that easy for her to do. They have a long slog ahead of them as a family."

"Okay. How about the clients we still have?" the Clinical Director asks pointedly.

"Well, the session with Lonnie and her husband went well, and I think the girls did just fine. It was good for them to see her looking so normal. I'm sure they enjoyed her ability to pay attention to them." Kym says.

"Lonnie mentioned her fears in women's group, afraid of what the girls might be thinking. But it sounds like they did okay – right?" Janet asks.

"Right. They're adorable. I also had a chance to meet with Cathy and her parents. I put out the theory that some of Cathy's behavior may be an attempt to test their attachment to her. It's not uncommon for adopted folks to have this impulse. When I was with the family, I could feel her parents' commitment, so when they've sent her away to the grandparents' it sound more protective of her than punitive. I feel encouraged for Cathy, if she'll let them in."

"I made some time with Cathy like Janet had encouraged me to do," Sarah shared. "We talked some more about your theory, and she mentioned that she had seen herself sabotage some of her friendships before. She just never put it together with an adoption issue. So I think you made a good call."

"She mentioned in women's group that she is really thinking

about it. Score one for the Family Counselor!" Janet says as she knuckle bumps Kym next to her.

Kym is grinning.

The team starts focusing on exit planning for Donna, when Janet notices the time and slips out to conduct Process Group.

Process Group

The clients are relatively on time. J.P. has eaten and has returned to his room. Janet has to admit she's relieved. She decides to open with her usual check in and see what's on their mind before asking Jesse to introduce a topic.

"I'm supposed to be exiting pretty soon, and I admit I'm getting a little nervous," Donna checks in. "This isn't my first rehab, and I am worried I'll blow it."

"I can relate," Angie says. "It's not mine either, and after watching three people blowup this weekend, I am scared that my emotions could get the better of me and I'll screw up too."

"That makes sense to me," Janet says. "When you think back to what happened before you picked up your first drink or drug after you were sober, do you see a clear pattern? We pick it up again as the last step in relapse, not the first."

"I can remember feeling angry all the time," Angie says. "My mom would ask me about it, and the reason I was so mad kept changing. Sometimes I would lose it in a store, and be mean to the cashier. Then I would be so embarrassed that I wouldn't go back there to shop."

"Have you always struggled with anger management?" Jesse asks.

"My mom says I've always had a temper. But I think it's gotten worse the older I get. It's really bad around my period. It's like I can't help myself – I go off on people."

"Have you ever seen an OB/GYN about it?" Janet asks.

The Work Goes On

"Not really. I just figured it's the way I am."

"I think it's worth talking to a doctor about, because it's really common and can be treated." Janet said. "I'll give you some contacts after group so you can make some calls and we can get you in before you leave treatment."

"I was wondering about that new drug, Campral," Donna asks

Jeff and Alan both chime in, "Yeah, we were talking about that during smoke break. Does it work?" Alan asks.

"Some clients have had good luck with it, it really helps ease out the cravings for alcohol and it's not as dangerous as antabuse." Janet explains

"I thought antabuse just made you sick?" Jeff says

Janet sees Jorge and another man walk by the group room door out of the corner of her eye. *"Oh, Johnson must be here,"* she thinks.

"Well it also makes your blood pressure spike and you can have stroke. So I only refer it as a last resort. The question is whether or not your insurance will cover Campral because it's still pretty expensive." Janet says.

"Well, I need all the help I can get," Donna retorts, "And so I'll spend what I need to spend if I can make my recovery work this time. I'm really tired of rehab, no offense,"

"None taken," Janet laughs. "I'd be tired too if I didn't get to go home every night!" she smiles.

The group hears J.P. talking and looks out the door to see him in handcuffs walking out with his P.O. Everyone stops talking and looks slightly alarmed.

Janet gets their attention. "I see J.P. is leaving with his parole officer. How're you guys doing with that?"

"Does he have to go to jail?" Alan asks.

"Why does he have to be handcuffed?" Cathy wonders.

The Work Goes On

"Well, its protocol that the P.O. has to handcuff him when transporting him, and yes, he will go back to jail until he's processed. How do you feel about that?" Jesse asks the group.

"I think it's really harsh," Cathy says. "I don't think you should've sent him back to jail." She says heatedly.

"Does it seem unfair to you? I know you hate it when things are unfair?'

"Yeah. You said addiction is a disease, so sending him to jail for drinking doesn't make sense."

"I get what you're saying, and I agree that jail is not the place for addicts. Our dilemma was that we had the threatening of Tony last week, and then we had the pruno that made both he and Jason very ill. The stability of the house has to come first." Janet says.

"So, what would I have to do to get thrown out?" Cathy asks. Janet knows this is a hot button issue for her, so speaks very carefully.

"Cathy, if your behavior was putting you at risk, we would be talking to you LONG before we got to the point where we would ask you to leave. There's a process before hand, and J.P. knew what it was. Sometimes people aren't ready to move forward in their lives and still need a time out. I promise we don't just throw you out without a warning and a request that you change whatever it is that is making you at risk."

Cathy was thinking about this explanation. *"God, I hope she trusts me enough."*

"That makes sense to me, actually" says Alan. "When there's too much drama it's hard to concentrate on our own recovery, right?"

"That's it exactly," Janet smiles.

"Are you going to throw Jason out?" Cathy asks.

"We're going to talk to Jason when he gets back and make the decision with him. He'll be included in the decision," Janet reassures her.

The group continues to process J.P. and their own relapse risk which was exactly what Janet had hoped would happen.

After Process Group Janet and Jesse return to the office where Ricardo lets them know that Jason is on his way from the hospital, so the Clinical Director is coming to participate in the conversation with Jason and his mother.

"How are the clients doing?" Ricardo checks in.

"They were a little shaken by the perp walk, but it lead to a great relapse prevention conversation," Jesse says.

Ricardo nodded. "Actually, the timing was pretty good. They were all in group."

Janet is working on her chart notes before the Clinical Director arrives. "Are we getting new clients tomorrow?" Janet asks as she types.

"It's your lucky day, Mamacita. We're getting two new state guys, one for each of us!" Ricardo teases her.

Janet makes a sight moan, "Oh, God."

Ricardo looks at Jesse, "Remember the time we had the guy make a homemade tattoo gun?"

"Yeah, he melted down the black checkers and mixed it with ink!" Jesse laughs.

"He gave another client the jankiest tattoo I've ever seen. I would've punched the guy in the mouth if someone in prison gave me a tattoo like that." Jorge says as he comes in the room. "Oh, the big guy is here," Jorge adds.

They hear the Clinical Director come in the front door and greet a couple of the clients as he heads into the office. "Hey, is Jason back yet?"

"Not yet," Ricardo says.

The Work Goes On

"How did it go with J.P.? Did Johnson make it during group?"

"He did. It went very smoothly," Jorge says.

The Clinical Director nods with satisfaction, and picks up the log to catch up on the day while he waits.

Jorge heads back out to the main area to check on the clients while Ricardo turns back to his screen. Jesse grabs Jeff's file and gets ready for his weekly one-on-one. He leaves to meet Jeff in the other counseling room.

Janet hears Jason's mom walking up the driveway with Jason following behind her, and the doorbell rings.

The Clinical Director greets them and invites them in for a conversation.

Jason

"So, Jason. Sounds like you had a rough night. How are you feeling now?" the Clinical Director asks.

"I'm doing better, sir. I didn't tear anything which is cool."

"What possessed you to drink J.P.'s pruno?"

"He told me during the day on Saturday that he was making it, and I kept thinking about it, thinking about it. I feel so anxious most of the time, worried about court, worried about finding a job. All I could think about is getting a break from my head. It never stops," Jason explains.

"How come you decided not to tell us?" Ricardo asks.

"Because you would have stopped us, and I really wanted to see what it would be like. It's all I could think about, really." Jason said quietly.

"What do you think we should do now?' Janet asks him.

"I'm not really sure. Obviously, I can't handle being around alcohol yet."

The Work Goes On

"What are his options?" Jason's mother asks.

"Well, we could discharge him to another program, or we could start him over in our program. Either way, I think he needs more time to stabilize," the Clinical Director explains.

"I don't want to start somewhere else. I already know everyone here!" Jason says to his mother.

"Well, if we go that route, we would have to charge a little more to extend his stay," the Clinical Director explains.

"I could do that, if I can make two separate payments," she says.

"We could easily do that, if that's what you want to do. It's one of the upsides of Non-profit!" the Clinical Directors smiles.

"I'm wondering about your anxiety, Jason," Janet says. "Maybe we should have you see our Psychologist and see if there may be something else going on with you that we need to address."

"You mean like medication?" his mother asks. "I'm hoping he gets off drugs and alcohol, so I'm worried about medication," she says.

"We would be cautious about it. Maybe he needs longer term counseling," Janet tells her. Jason and his mother both nod in agreement.

They conclude the meeting, and Jason goes into the dining area to see the other clients who welcome him back gladly.

Janet logs the meeting and then charts the meeting in Jason's chart, and the Clinical Director heads back to the administrative office.

Janet has decided to wait to talk to Eddie until he arrives for his shift, so is glad to see him appear a little early.

Eddie

"Hi, Eddie. Want to go grab some coffee and sit outside for a minute?" Janet asks.

"Sure thing," he says following her to the kitchen.

Outside on the bench Janet opens the conversation. "Eddie, I noticed that you called in last Friday, and you look a little quiet today. Are you feeling okay? I was wondering if adding Sarah to your shift might have thrown you for a loop."

"I'm okay, I guess. Honestly, I don't feel as confident if you guys feel like Sarah needs to babysit me. I know I relapsed awhile back, but I thought I had proven that I was pretty stable again. I'm going to my meetings, meeting with my sponsor-"

"I know," Janet interrupts. "I was afraid you were thinking that. We wanted to keep Sarah's skills up until we have a counselor position for her. We've been thinking about opening an Outpatient program, and I want her to be able to transition if that happens. It's not about you at all."

"I know the Clinical Director said something about that, but I didn't really believe him."

"Why, you know he's a straight shooter? The guy doesn't have any tact so if it was about you, he would have said so!" Janet laughs.

Eddie smiles, "Okay, I guess that's true. I'm not sure how I'm supposed to work her in. Should we share the group, trade off?"

"I think you know best. You have been running the night program for awhile now and know the flow of the evening. I can imagine you could use her help with processing sometimes, or maybe to help you work the room when they are doing group exercises. It would be really good to have her to do female UA's if necessary."

"That's true. I've worried about that, since it's usually me and Jorge."

"Exactly. I promise, it is not about watching you, or making sure you do what you're supposed to. It really is about using her skills now that she has graduated from school."

"Okay," Eddie looks relieved. "I feel better about it. It's going to be okay."

"Actually, I'm hoping it will be better than okay, and that you'll actually enjoy having someone to work with – share the charting with."

"Ooooh, I hadn't thought of that. That is a serious upside," Eddie laughs.

Janet

Janet made it to her therapy about 5 minutes late due to her talk with Eddie, but it was worth it. She also felt more at ease now that she had followed her instincts and connected with him.

"I went to Al-anon, and I realized how messed up I really am!" Janet laughs.

"What did you hear that gave you that impression?" her therapist wonders.

"It's not so much what I heard, but how similar we all are. In a way, it was good to be amongst 'my people,' like I felt in A.A. Only these guys are all about relationships. I realized listening to them that I've got a long way to go before I'm going to be ready to trust anyone enough to get close to them again."

"Do you see any positive side to allowing it?'

"Not at the moment, if I'm honest. But I'm going to trust that there's more here than I can see because I have a blind spot. I feel safe hiding in the television and my routines. I feel safe providing support to other people, and at the same time not having to risk intimacy."

"Are you ever lonely?'

"Sometimes. I get aware that I have a hole where David used to be, and I wish I could fill it. But since I want to fill it with him, and that's not possible, I sort of accept it as remaining empty. I can't imagine filling it with anyone but him yet."

"That's okay. Maybe someday it will seem like a realistic option.

The Work Goes On

In the meantime we'll keep working on your relationship with yourself, okay?" the therapist smiles.

www.ingramcontent.com/pod-product-compliance
Lightning Source LLC
Chambersburg PA
CBHW031645040426
42453CB00006B/217